Delivering Adult Learning – Level 3 Coursebook

Ann Gravells

Learning Matters

First published in 2006 by Learning Matters Ltd.

British Library Cataloguing in Publication Data
A CIP record for this book is available from the British Library.

ISBN-13: 978 1 84445 064 0
ISBN-10: 1 84445 064 3

Cover design by Topics – The Creative Partnership
Project management by Deer Park Productions, Tavistock, Devon
Typeset by Pantek Arts Ltd, Maidstone, Kent
Printed and bound in Great Britain by Ashford Colour Press Ltd, Gosport, Hampshire

Learning Matters Ltd
33 Southernhay East
Exeter EX1 1NX
Tel: 01392 215560
Email: info@learningmatters.co.uk
www.learningmatters.co.uk

CONTENTS

ACKNOWLEDGEMENTS

I would like to thank the following for their support and encouragement whilst I was writing this book:

Pat Barylski

Jennifer Clark

Angela Faulkner

Peter Frankish

Bob Gravells

Chris Letza

Julia Morris

Dan O'Connor

Sarah Preston

Susan Simpson

The students and staff of the teacher/training department at Bishop Burton College and my colleagues at City & Guilds.

Whilst the chapters have been cross referenced to the City & Guilds Certificate and Diploma in Delivering Learning, and the International Certificate and Diploma in Teaching and Supporting Learners, the City and Guilds of London Institute accepts no liability for the contents of this book.

Ann Gravells is a lecturer in teacher training at Bishop Burton College in East Yorkshire. She has over 21 years' experience of delivering learning.

She is also a consultant to City & Guilds for various projects and recently co-wrote the 7302 Certificate and Diploma in Delivering Learning and the International Certificate and Diploma in Teaching and Supporting Learners. She also externally verifies the City & Guilds teacher/training qualifications.

Ann is involved with the development of the new Lifelong Learning (LLUK) Initial Award standards.

Ann holds a Degree in Education, a PGCE and is currently working towards her Master's in Educational Management.

In this chapter you will cover the following topics.

- Introduction to the book and how to use it;
- Skills needed to effectively deliver learning;
- Progression;
- FENTO/LLUK standards.

Introduction to the book and how to use it

Congratulations upon making the decision to work towards a Level 3 teaching/training qualification – the start of a rewarding career delivering learning.

Alternatively, you might not wish to take a qualification, but want more information about how to effectively deliver learning, for example, in your place of work if you train people as part of their working role, either in groups or as individuals.

The book is structured in chapters which relate to the full process of delivering learning. This is often referred to as the *training cycle*. You can work logically through the book or just look up relevant aspects within the chapters.

There are activities to enable you to think about how you deliver learning, and examples to help you understand the process.

At the end of each chapter is a theory focus, enabling you to research relevant topics further.

Each chapter is cross-referenced to the units of the City & Guilds 7302 Certificate and Diploma in Delivering Learning, the National Vocational Qualification (NVQ) Level 3 in Learning and Development and the City & Guilds International Certificate and Diploma in Teaching and Supporting Learners.

If you are delivering learning internationally, some of the regulations and bodies referred to in the book may only be applicable to the United Kingdom.

At the back of the book there is a useful list of acronyms.

The appendices contain a full cross-referencing grid to the Level 3 standards, useful pro-formas and a delivery checklist.

The index will help you quickly locate useful topics.

Skills needed to effectively deliver learning

You will need subject skills; for example, you may have a hobby and wish to develop this further to train others. You may already be delivering learning and have a qualification in your subject area, but may need to update this perhaps due to changes in technology.

Depending on the subject you wish to deliver, the qualifications you need to have, and the professional updating you may need to carry out, will differ.

You will need a reasonable level of literacy and numeracy; these are part of *skills for life*. If you give a handout containing spelling mistakes, your students will think the spelling mistakes are correct just because you are a tutor. You may need to take further qualifications as you progress with your career. This could be due to changes in legislation or external or awarding body requirements. It is also useful to have information and communication technology (ICT) skills. You can then design professional presentations and handouts. Some organisations now use electronic registers and communicate mainly by e-mail. Often, the organisations' policies and procedures are on their intranet, rather than in hard copy format.

Some of the skills and attributes you may already have, or need to develop, include being:

- adaptive
- articulate
- assertive
- charismatic
- committed
- communicative
- competent
- conciliatory
- confident
- creative
- decisive
- dedicated
- determined
- diplomatic
- empathic
- energetic
- enthusiastic
- flexible
- focused
- honest
- intelligent
- organised
- patient
- persistent
- positive
- professional
- realistic
- receptive
- reliable
- respectful
- responsible
- responsive
- trustworthy.

Progression

Once you have successfully completed your Level 3 course, you might wish to progress further with your career. If you are teaching or training on programmes which receive funding, you may need to work towards a Level 4 qualification. Examples are the Certificate in Education, or if you have a degree you may be able to take the Post Graduate Certificate in Education (PGCE) or the City & Guilds Certificate in Further Education Teaching (7407).

It is likely that from September 2007 all new tutors, trainers and teachers in England will need to meet qualification requirements described in the Department for Education and Skills (DfES) publication *Equipping our Teachers for the Future: Reforming Initial Teacher Training for the Learning and Skills Sector.*

FENTO/LLUK standards

New standards for teaching, tutoring and training are currently under development to underpin a new framework of approved qualifications to support competence and capability in learning delivery roles. There will be an *Initial Award* at Level 3 and higher-level awards leading to *Qualified Teacher Learning and Skills* (QTLS).

The Further Education National Training Organisation (FENTO) is now incorporated into Lifelong Learning UK (LLUK). It is the body responsible for the professional development of all those working in further education, work-based learning, higher education, community learning and development, libraries, archives and information services.

The standards currently address the professional development of those people who deliver learning rather than the development of their subject expertise and were designed to raise standards in further education.

Summary

In this chapter you have covered:

● Introduction to the book and how to use it;

● Skills needed to effectively deliver learning;

● Progression;

● FENTO/LLUK standards.

Theory focus

Websites

Department for Education and Skills – dfes.gov.uk

Lifelong Learning UK – lifelonglearninguk.org

City and Guilds – cityandguilds.com

Introduction

In this chapter you will cover the following points.

- What is adult learning?;
- What can you deliver?;
- How can you deliver?;
- Roles and functions of the tutor;
- The role of external and awarding bodies;
- Delivering to different age groups;
- Different levels and types of courses/qualifications;
- Challenges, barriers and attitudes to learning;
- Health and safety considerations;
- Entitlement, equality, inclusivity and diversity.

There are activities and examples to help you reflect on the above which will assist your understanding of the process of delivering learning.

This chapter contributes towards the knowledge and skills required for the City & Guilds 7302 Certificate in Delivering Learning: An Introduction:

→ Unit 1 – Key principles of delivering learning

→ Unit 2 – Learning programmes

→ Unit 5 - Case study.

This chapter contributes towards the knowledge and skills required for the City & Guilds 7302 Diploma in Delivering Learning:

→ Unit 2 – Designing learning programmes

→ Unit 7 – Professional development.

This chapter contributes towards the knowledge and understanding required for the National Vocational Qualification (NVQ) in Learning and Development Level 3:

(→) L9 – Create a climate that promotes learning.

This chapter contributes towards the knowledge and skills required for the International City & Guilds Certificate and Diploma in Teaching and Supporting Learners:

(→) Unit 1 – Identifying learners' needs

(→) Unit 3 – Delivering learning.

What is adult learning?

Learning is all about helping someone reach their full potential, whether this is for personal or professional reasons. You can help make a difference to someone's life and this can be very rewarding.

Adult learning can take place in a variety of contexts; for example, further education colleges, work-based, adult and community learning centres, private training organisations, the forces, the National Health Service, industry and commerce.

Adults are usually motivated to learn, either for their own personal benefit or to enhance their job role. This motivation ensures they are keen and enthusiastic students, usually attending their training voluntarily, often in their own time. They are eager to learn new skills and knowledge.

Adults tend to have a lot of experience, whether it is practical or theoretical, and are used to being active and having self-discipline when it comes to learning. Adults are more confident to ask questions and challenge theories; they like to relate new learning to their own situations. If you are asked a question you cannot answer, say you will find out, and make sure you do. Whilst you are expected to have an in-depth knowledge of your subject, you won't know everything and it's best to be honest and admit when you don't know something.

Usually adults are not afraid of making a mistake. They have probably heard the phrase 'you learn from your mistakes'. They have learnt this through experience. Adults are often keen to tell you and the group of their experiences and how they have learnt from them.

When delivering learning, plan tasks in a logical order, relating theory to practice and involve students with discussions of their own experiences. Always state clearly what you are going to do and why. Recap and summarise topics, repeat key words and ask questions to check learning. Try not to do too much or complicate your delivery as new knowledge takes time to be assimilated. Keep things simple.

Adults will usually arrive on time, have the necessary materials, e.g. pens and paper, and not be disruptive. However, you need to consider their personal circumstances and situations especially if you are delivering an evening class and some of your students have been at work all day.

If a student does arrive a little late, smile and welcome them, give them time to settle down and tell them what you are doing at the moment. You can say you will catch up with them later. Try not to make them feel unwelcome or uncomfortable just because they are late. Keep them involved, don't make an example of them or they may decide not to return.

You can be on first-name terms with adults and have a more informal delivery style (depending upon your subject). Treat adults as adults – they are not children and will not tolerate you treating them as such. They may have had bad experiences at school which have stayed with them and could affect their current learning. Treat them as individuals, using their names and including them all in discussions and activities. Wherever possible, try to use practical activities to maintain interest and motivation. If you need to set any homework or assignments, make sure you give clear target dates and let them know if these dates can be extended or not. Adults have so many other responsibilities in their lives that time goes quickly and homework becomes a lesser priority. If you only see your students once a week, perhaps a phone call or an e-mail in between to check their progress can act as a useful prompt.

Activity

Think back to when you attended school and compare this to a more recent learning experience as an adult. How were you treated as a child at school? How were you treated as an adult more recently? Why do you think this was?

As an adult, you were probably given more responsibility and trust. You were treated with respect, and given credit for your experiences.

All students require boundaries and rules within which to work. These must be made clear early on in the course; they could be set by your organisation and/or produced by yourself. Setting ground rules will help everyone know their limits. Students like routine and will expect you to be organised and professional. Always start a session on time, stating what is going to be delivered, recapping points along the way and summarising at the end is a useful approach.

Activity

Imagine you have a new group of 15 students. You have decided to let them agree their own ground rules. If the group take ownership for their own rules, they are more likely to keep to them. What would you like them to decide?

Your response as a tutor might be based upon a previous course you have attended as a student, where you were, or were not, given any ground rules. Without ground rules, disruption may occur and affect the learning of your students.

Example

A group of adult students are taking a course in art and design. They have agreed the following ground rules:

- *arrive on time;*
- *switch off mobile phones;*
- *be polite and courteous to other students and the tutor;*
- *don't eat or drink in class;*
- *listen attentively;*
- *return punctually from breaks.*

Having ground rules gives a firm boundary for all students to work within. Often, if a ground rule is broken, it is the other students that will reprimand the offender, saving you the job.

What can you deliver?

If you are new to delivering learning, this could be because you are contemplating a change of career. You might not yet have a subject you would like to deliver and just want to know what it's like to teach before you make this decision.

Perhaps you have a hobby you would like to teach others; you know you are good at it and feel you have a lot of experience and knowledge you could pass on.

Activity

Think of a subject you would like to deliver. What skills and knowledge do you already have to enable you to effectively deliver this subject? What further training and/or qualifications do you think you may need?

If you are currently teaching, your methods might be based on experiences of how others have done it, or your own ideas. You might now feel you would like to deliver learning in a more professional manner.

You might be giving one-to-one support to others at home, in the workplace or in an educational setting or be a technician who demonstrates things to others in a variety of contexts.

Whatever has made you decide to deliver learning, you will need a specialist subject. Whilst this book will guide you through the process of delivering learning, it is up to you to ensure you are up to date with your subject knowledge.

Depending upon where and what you are going to deliver, you may not need to be qualified in your subject, but demonstrate appropriate experience and knowledge.

Example

Les has always been keen on gardening and has worked part time in a garden centre for the past six years. He feels he has the skills and ability to pass on his knowledge and experience to others. After approaching the local further education college, they have agreed to employ him to deliver one evening class per week. The evening class does not lead to a qualification, it is a course aimed at keen gardeners. The college has asked Les to enrol on a Level 3 course in Delivering Learning to help him plan and manage his delivery of the course. If his own delivery is successful, the college would like Les to offer a Level 1 Certificate in Horticulture next term. He will then need to take the Level 2 Certificate in Horticulture himself.

It is important to keep up to date with your subject specialism. There are often changes regarding external and awarding body requirements and technology. You could subscribe to trade journals, research via the Internet, attend courses and network with others. This is called *continuing professional development* (CPD).

How can you deliver?

Learning should be fun, enjoyable and challenging to the student. It should also be enjoyable and satisfying for you. To see someone carry out a task that you have taught them is very rewarding, especially if they had no prior knowledge or experience before meeting you.

To deliver learning effectively involves not only the way you deliver your subject, but many other factors that go before and after the delivery. This includes planning your sessions, preparing your delivery materials, assessing your students and evaluating yourself and your delivery.

When delivering learning, your personality and mannerisms will no doubt come across to your students as you deliver. You may do things you are not aware of, for example waving your arms around or fidgeting with a pen. It is really useful to make a visual recording of your delivery so that you can watch yourself afterwards. You may see things you didn't realise you did.

If you are new to delivering learning, you may find you are delivering in the same way you were taught at school or college. This could be lecturing, reading from a book or writing information on a board. You won't yet know all the other methods you could use to make learning interesting and involve the students actively. Active learning helps people remember, passive learning may lead to them forget. As you become more experienced at delivering learning, your confidence will grow and you will be able to experiment with different delivery methods.

Activity

Think of a recent learning experience and ask yourself the following questions.

What was good about it and why?

What wasn't so good and why?

Did you like the subject but not the tutor?

Did you like the tutor but not the subject?

Was the tutor well prepared, on time and professional with their delivery and approach?

Was it interesting and relevant to you?

Your responses will help you appreciate how a tutor can help deliver an effective session.

Roles and functions of the tutor

Depending upon where and what you are going to deliver, there are many roles and functions you will need to carry out. These might include:

- completing attendance records;
- maintaining records of student progress;
- having a duty of care for your students;
- inducting students to the organisation and course;
- carrying out one-to-one tutorials and reviews with students;
- following professional values and ethics;
- acting and speaking appropriately;
- standardising your practice with others;
- attending meetings;
- preparing delivery material and marking work;
- attending promotional events and exhibitions;
- referring students to other people or agencies when necessary.

When you start work as a tutor, you should receive an induction to the organisation and your role and responsibilities. You might have a *mentor*, someone who can help and support you. If you are unsure of anything, always ask.

Activity

Imagine you have just started a role as a part-time tutor in a community setting. What would you need to know before you started this role?

Your responses might show that you are asking questions like 'is there a syllabus for my course?', 'are there any assignments I need to use?', 'which room will I be teaching in?', 'what resources are available for me to use?', 'when can I give the group a break?', 'where are the toilets?'

You may have come up with many more questions. These are all things you need to know, and probably things your students will need to know too.

Your role as a deliverer of learning may be called something other than tutor; some examples are:

- assessor;
- coach;
- counsellor;
- facilitator;
- instructor;
- lecturer;
- mentor;
- teacher;
- trainer.

Your students may also be called something other than 'student'; some examples are:

- apprentice;
- candidate;
- learner;
- participant;
- pupil;
- trainee.

The role of external and awarding bodies

The Qualifications and Curriculum Authority (QCA) in England is a public body sponsored by the Department for Education and Skills (DfES) who accredit and monitor all qualifications in further and adult education and at work. If you are teaching towards a recognised qualification, it will have been approved by the QCA. The other regulatory authorities are Awdurdod Cymwysterau, Cwricwlwm ac Asesu Cymru in Wales (ACCAC), Council for the Curriculum, Examinations and Assessment in Northern Ireland (CCEA) and the Scottish Qualifications Authority in Scotland (SQA).

Once a qualification is approved, an awarding body can then certificate it, for example the Level 3 Certificate in Delivering Learning has been accredited by City & Guilds.

An awarding body issues certificates for accredited courses. The awarding body will monitor the delivery of the course, a process often called *external verification* or *external moderation*. If your students will be taking an examination, this will be at a date and time approved by the awarding body and will need to be conducted according to their procedures.

If you deliver a course that is a National Vocational Qualification (NVQ), a National Training Organisation (NTO) or Sector Skills Council (SSC) will have developed the standards that make up the qualification.

External bodies include the Adult Learning Inspectorate (ALI) who are the inspectorate for skills, workforce development and preparation for employment.

The Office for Standards in Education (Ofsted) is the inspectorate for children and adult learners in England. It is their job to contribute to the provision of better education and care through effective inspection and regulation of funded programmes.

If you deliver learning in a college, training organisation or the workplace, it is likely you will be inspected at some time.

If you are delivering learning internationally, different regulations may apply.

Change is inevitable in education. Your subject area may be experiencing new developments and it is essential to keep up with what's happening. External and awarding bodies produce guidance which will help you.

Delivering to different age groups

You may be asked to deliver learning to young people as well as adults. You may need to modify your delivery style and methods from those used with adults.

You may be delivering in a school environment and have to follow their rules and regulations. On the other hand, the students may come to your educational organisation and therefore act differently in this environment from the way they would at school. They may behave in a more mature manner if given responsibility, or they may act over-confidently in front of their peers.

The 14–16 age group are still attending compulsory education in the United Kingdom. This may bring with it issues that you will have to deal with such as poor behaviour, truancy, peer pressure, disruption and bullying. You will need patience and understanding and must treat those in the group as individuals, remaining firm but fair to all.

Ensuring your sessions are meaningful, with lots of interesting practical tasks, will help classroom control. If you can't use practical tasks, break your session down into lots of smaller aspects, recapping each before moving on. Never assume or underestimate your students' knowledge. Younger students need lots of praise and encouragement, they appreciate you listening to them and supporting them when necessary. If you ask a student a question and they answer wrongly, don't dismiss this, but try to relate their answer to a real situation which is relevant to the subject. Include all students when asking questions and use their names. Make them feel their contribution is valued. If you are enthusiastic about the subject, hopefully they will be.

The 16–19 age group in the United Kingdom are not in compulsory education, but some students could be attending a course as part of an apprenticeship programme. Non-attendance may affect their funding allowance. Some problems that you may encounter with the 14–16 age range may also be encountered with the 16–19 age range.

You may be teaching a broad spectrum of ages. All students have experiences they bring with them to the session and they need to be treated as individuals and with respect.

Example

You are delivering a two-hour information technology course which lasts ten weeks. There are ten students aged from 16 to 65. As part of the first session you asked them all to introduce themselves and say a little about their experience of computers. You soon realise the older students have very minimal experience: three have never switched on a computer before. The younger students are more confident and have used computers at school. You therefore decide to sit a younger student next to an older one so they can help and support each other. Each student will be working individually through a series of tasks, at their own pace. You will move around the room, giving each student individual support. During the times you are not with them, they can ask each other questions rather than sitting waiting for you.

Depending upon your subject, you will find your own ways to reach each individual, giving them confidence to progress with their learning. Always give positive encouragement to retain motivation and treat all student questions as valid, no matter how silly they may seem to you at the time.

Learning is for life, and should continue after the post-compulsory stage. The term 'lifelong learning' is often used today to denote this. Learning should take into account the students', employers' and community's needs. It should also take into account any spiritual, moral, social and cultural needs.

Different levels and types of courses/ qualifications

Not all courses lead to qualifications; some are for leisure or work-related skills. Those that do lead to qualifications are classed as general, vocational or occupational.

Example

Leisure

Rob has not attended any courses since leaving school 12 years ago. He wishes to learn how to use a computer; his local community centre is running a one-day course for beginners. He will attend the course to gain the confidence he needs to use his home computer. He will not be taking an assessment or exam but does receive a certificate of attendance.

Example

Work-related

Julie works for a large company which has just updated their quality-assurance procedures. She will attend a four-hour course delivered by her employer to update her knowledge. She will then apply this knowledge to her job role. She will not take an examination or receive a certificate of attendance.

Example

General

Danielle left school two years ago but did not achieve many qualifications. She is going to attend two evening classes a week at a further education college. This will lead to a General Certificate of Secondary Education (GCSE) in English and an Advanced (A) level in maths. She will complete course work and take an examination.

Example

Vocational

Razia is 16 years old and wishes to take a subject that will relate to his future career. He has chosen to take a General National Vocational Qualification (GNVQ) in Catering. He is also taking Key Skills. These are skills in communication, application of numbers, and information technology. They have been designed to improve employability skills.

Example

Occupational

Peter has just stared work full time as a trainee hairdresser. He is working towards his National Vocational Qualification (NVQ) in Hairdressing. He will be assessed on the job and will not need to take an examination. He will be able to work at his own pace and receive training and assessment in his place of work.

The national qualifications framework (NQF) for England, Wales and Northern Ireland sets out the levels at which qualifications are recognised. It helps students make decisions about the qualifications they need, by comparing the levels of different qualifications and identifying clear progression routes to their chosen career.

The three regulatory authorities have recently revised the NQF and the number of levels has increased to nine (Entry level, plus Levels 1 to 8).

Challenges, barriers and attitudes to learning

When delivering learning, you will face many challenges. Some of these will be from the students, for example, their behaviour; others may be from your organisation, for example, a lack of resources.

Some students will have barriers to learning that may affect their attendance, perhaps due to transport problems or childcare arrangements.

Some students may have limited basic skills such as literacy and numeracy, and this may affect their confidence.

Attitudes to learning are often based upon previous learning experiences, whether good or bad. You need to reassure your students that you will help make their learning a positive and rewarding one. Communication is the key. You may be delivering to a group or on a one-to-one basis. Discussing any worries or concerns your students might have, and letting them know they can talk to you and, that you will listen, will help with their learning experience.

Examples of challenges and barriers include:

- awareness of financial support;
- cultural and language differences;
- disabilities/age/medical problems;
- discipline, behaviour and attendance;
- emotional or psychological problems;
- family commitments;
- lack of confidence and/or motivation;
- lack of resources;
- lack of support;
- mixed ability learning styles;
- peer pressure;
- people's fears: technology, change, learning;
- personal/work circumstances;
- previous learning experiences;
- status of the group – hierarchy of staff that may work together;
- the environment;
- the weather;
- timing issues;
- transport.

Depending upon the challenges and barriers, ways to overcome these may include:

- being honest – if you don't know something, be honest and say you will find out, then make sure you do;

- being positive and enthusiastic – this should rub off on your students;

- communicating effectively – involving students actively and listening to what they have to say;

- giving ongoing constructive and positive feedback;

- having support strategies in place, e.g. one-to-one support if a student has missed a session;

- carrying out initial assessment – to find out what students know already in order to have a logical progression;

- ascertaining learning styles – to know how students learn in order to adapt your delivery methods to suit;

- negotiation skills – to help agree their programme of learning;

- setting clear aims and objectives – involving the group to realise they will benefit in the long term;

- involving the students – get them to carry out research and present their findings so they feel a part of the learning process;

- presentation methods – plan carefully to make learning interesting and fun, use several delivery methods to cover all learning styles;

- adapting your delivery methods and resources where necessary to suit any particular student needs, e.g. visual impairment, dyslexia, etc.;

- remembering student names and using them whenever possible;

- suitability of environment – to use all rooms and facilities available;

- valuing the contribution of all students.

Example

You are due to deliver a course which commences at 6 pm on a Monday evening. At the first session, three out of the ten students are a little late. You find out this is due to transport problems. As a group, you decide to start the class at 6.15 pm and end a quarter of an hour later.

Health and safety considerations

Students are entitled to learn in a safe and healthy environment. Health and safety is your responsibility as well as your organisation's. If you see a potential hazard, do something about it; don't wait for an accident to happen.

You may be using electrical equipment; this will need regular checks by your organisation to ensure it is safe. Your students may need to wear protective clothing for some activities.

Example

Think about the subject you would like to teach. What health and safety considerations might there be when delivering learning?

Your response may include the environment within which you will be teaching, for example ventilation, heating, lighting and use of electrical equipment. You also need to ensure that any floor surfaces are not slippery, that any trailing wires are out of the way and any equipment the students will be working with is safe and reliable.

If you are delivering a subject that may be dangerous or hazardous, you may need to carry out risk assessments which will need to be documented.

You will need to know your organisation's accident and fire procedures such as the location of fire exits, extinguishers and first aid facilities. You should inform your students of these. If you have any students who commence your course late, you should always give them this information. You could include it in an induction handout or it may already be in your organisation's handbook.

You should also familiarise yourself with your organisation's Health and Safety Policy and the relevant government or local legislation. You may have students who have individual needs such as epilepsy or diabetes. It is important to know who they are and what you need to do in case of an emergency.

Entitlement, equality, inclusivity and diversity

All students are entitled to be treated with respect and dignity. Everyone is an individual, with different experiences, abilities and needs. As a tutor, you need to take all this into account when delivering learning and ensure you give equal support to all your students, without favouritism. You should not discriminate in any way and you may have to challenge your own values, attitudes and beliefs so that you are not imposing these upon your students.

The same will apply to your students, you need to ensure they are treating each other fairly and not harassing others.

The Disability Discrimination Act (1995) has made it law that all students must be given the necessary adaptations needed to allow them to fully participate in their learning.

If you are delivering learning internationally, there will be different regulations you may need to follow.

Inclusiveness is a core value underpinning the Further Education National Training Organisation's (FENTO) standards:

> Equality of opportunity is a crucial foundation upon which good teaching, learning and assessment is based. All learners should have access to appropriate educational opportunities regardless of ethnic origin, gender, age, sexual orientation or degree of learning disability and/or difficulty. Consequently, the values of entitlement, equality and inclusiveness are of fundamental importance to teachers and teaching teams.

Diversity is about valuing the differences in people, whether that relates to gender, race, age, disability or any other individual characteristics they may have.

Activity

You are due to deliver a flower arranging course to a group of 18 adult students. You have been informed two students are wheelchair users. What would you need to check before they arrive?

Your responses probably included checking access to the building and to toilets and refreshment areas. You would also need to ensure the furniture is suitable, for example, the height of the tables and that there is room to manoeuvre wheelchairs around.

The best way to address inclusivity and diversity is to ask your students what *they* feel their needs are. You can then address their individual needs knowing you are doing what is right for them, not just what you *think* is right.

Summary

In this chapter you have covered:

- What is adult learning?;
- What can you deliver?;
- How can you deliver?;
- Roles and functions of the tutor;
- The role of external and awarding bodies;

- Delivering to different age groups;

- Different levels and types of courses/qualifications;

- Challenges, barriers and attitudes to learning;

- Health and safety considerations;

- Entitlement, equality, inclusivity and diversity.

Theory focus
Books

Daines JW et al (2002) *Adult Learning, Adult Teaching*, 3rd edition, Welsh Academic Press.

Minton D (2005) *Teaching Skills in Further and Adult Education*, 3rd edition, Thomson Learning.

Reece I, Walker S (2003) *Teaching, Training and Learning*, 5th edition, Business Education Publishers Ltd.

Wallace S (2005) *Teaching and Supporting Learning in Further Education*, 2nd edition, Learning Matters Ltd.

Websites

Adult Learning Inspectorate – ali.gov.uk

Awdurdod Cymwysterau, Cwricwlwm ac Asesu Cymru – accac.org.uk

Commission for Racial Equality – cre.gov.uk

City & Guilds – cityandguilds.com

Council for the Curriculum, Examinations and Assessment in Northern Ireland – ccea.org.uk

Department for Education and Skills – dfes.gov.uk and teachernet.gov.uk

Disability Rights Commission – drc.gb.org

Disability Government Site – direct.gov.uk

Education and Learning Wales – elwa.org.uk

Educational Theory – businessballs.com

English and Maths online testing – move-on.org.uk

Equal Opportunities Commission – eoc.org.uk

Health and Safety Executive – hse.gov.uk

Learning and Skills Council – lsc.gov.uk

Learning and Skills Network – lsneducation.org.uk

Lifelong Learning UK (LLUK) – lifelonglearninguk.org

Lifelong Learning – lifelonglearning.co.uk

National Institute of Adult Continuing Education – niace.org.uk

National Programme for Specialist Leaders of Behaviour and Attendance – teachernet.gov.uk/wholeschool/behaviour/npsl_ba/

Office for Standards in Education – ofsted.gov.uk

Qualifications and Curriculum Authority – qca.org.uk

Scottish Qualifications Authority – sqa.org.uk

Scottish Enterprise – scottish-enterprise.com

Sector Skills Development Agencies – ssda.org.uk

Support for Learning – support4learning.org.uk

Times Educational Supplement – tes.co.uk

Workers Educational Association – wea.org.uk

2 KEY PRINCIPLES OF LEARNING

Introduction

In this chapter you will cover the following points.

- Theories regarding principles of learning;
- The training cycle;
- Learning styles;
- Domains of learning;
- Motivation;
- Pedagogical and andragogical models of learning.

There are activities and examples to help you reflect on the above which will assist your understanding of the key principles of learning.

This chapter contributes towards the knowledge and skills required for the City & Guilds 7302 Certificate in Delivering Learning: An Introduction:

→ Unit 1 – Key principles of delivering learning.

This chapter contributes towards the knowledge and skills required for the City & Guilds 7302 Diploma in Delivering Learning:

→ Unit 1 – Principles of delivering learning

→ Unit 9 – Professional practice – case study.

This chapter contributes towards the knowledge and understanding required for the National Vocational Qualification (NVQ) in Learning and Development Level 3:

→ L9 – Create a climate that promotes learning

→ L12 – Enable individual learning through coaching

(→) L13 – Enable group learning

(→) L18 – Respond to changes in learning and development.

This chapter contributes towards the knowledge and skills required for the International City & Guilds Certificate and Diploma in Teaching and Supporting Learners:

(→) Unit 1 – Identifying learners' needs.

Theories regarding principles of learning

There are lots of examples of theories or ideas regarding how people learn. These ideas will have been based on thoughts and experiences. Some are quite old theories, but are tried and trusted; others are fairly recent. You may even come up with your own theories or challenge existing ones. All people learn differently, perhaps influenced by experiences in their childhood, school, personal or professional relationships.

Activity

Think back to something you have learnt recently. Did you attend a course or learn it yourself? Were you attentive whilst the tutor was explaining it and did you understand what they said? Could you then apply this learning to a situation relevant to you?

If you paid attention and understood the subject, whether it was practical or theoretical, you would probably make a change to your behaviour.

When you learn something, you will probably adapt, change or modify your behaviour as a result.

The way people learn varies but can be based upon the following theories which you may like to research further.

Sensory theory

Using the senses – sight, hearing, touch, smell and taste – will enable you to learn and remember. Laird (1985) suggests learning occurs when the senses are stimulated.

Laird's theory suggests that if multi-senses are stimulated, greater learning takes place. You could therefore adapt your delivery styles and resources to enable your students to use as many of their senses as possible.

Example

When you were a child, if you saw something that interested you, you would touch it, probably putting it in your mouth if it was small, shaking it to hear if it made a noise and putting it near your nose to smell. You would soon learn if something tasted nasty not to put it in your mouth again. Therefore, a change in your behaviour took place as a result.

Experiential theory

This theory refers to the process by which people understand their experiences, and as a result, modify their behaviour. It is based on the idea that the more often we reflect on a task, the more often we have the opportunity to modify and refine our efforts.

People learn through four distinct processes, often developing one method of learning more than another. Kolb (1984) proposed a four-stage learning process with a cycle of learning, through:

- concrete experience;
- observation and reflection;
- abstract conceptualisation;
- active experimentation.

Concrete experience is about experiencing or immersing yourself in the task and is the first stage in which a person simply carries out the task assigned. This is the *doing* stage.

Observation and reflection involve stepping back from the task and reviewing what has been done and experienced. Your values, attitudes and beliefs can influence your thinking at this stage. This is the *thinking about what you have done stage*.

Abstract conceptualisation involves interpreting the events that have been carried out and understanding the relationships among them. This is the *planning how you will do it differently stage*.

Active experimentation enables you to take the new learning and predict what is likely to happen next or what actions should be taken to refine the way the task is done again. This is the *redoing* stage based upon experience and reflection.

The process of learning can begin at any stage and is continuous, i.e. there is no limit to the number of cycles you can make in a learning situation. This theory suggests that without reflection, people would continue to repeat their mistakes.

Example

Wang is taking a course in word processing which has an examination at the end. If he fails he will not know why he has failed. He will need to wait another year before he can re-take the examination. During the course, he could experience the learning process, but not reflect upon what he might be doing wrong that may lead to him failing the examination. He therefore could not modify his behaviour and try again. If he took a course with ongoing assessment instead of an examination at the end, he would have the opportunity to go through the full cycle. He would have the experience, reflect upon it due to ongoing feedback, think how he could improve and then experiment to try again.

You may have heard the saying 'you learn by experience'. You might find that doing a task, then thinking about it, leads you to plan how you would do it differently next time. Repeating tasks will help your students learn, whether this is a practical task or a theoretical subject.

Humanist theory

This theory suggests that learning will take place if the person delivering it acts as a facilitator. They should establish an atmosphere in which their students feel comfortable and able to discuss new ideas if they are not threatened by external factors. Rogers (1983) and others have developed the theory of *facilitative learning*. This is based upon a belief that people have a natural eagerness to learn and that learning involves changing your own concept of yourself.

Example

You are taking a new group for a subject you haven't delivered before. You have planned what you are going to deliver and how you are going to do this. However, your students will also have expectations regarding what they want to learn. Their ideas may differ from yours. You therefore decide to ask them at the first session what they expect from the course. This will enable you to plan your delivery to cover their expectations, not just around what you want to deliver.

Behaviourist theory

Giving immediate feedback whether positive or negative, will enable a student to behave in a certain way. Skinner (1974) believed that behaviour is a function of its consequences. The student will repeat the desired behaviour if positive reinforcement follows. If negative feedback is given, the behaviour should not be repeated.

Positive reinforcement or rewards can include verbal feedback such as 'That's great, you've produced that document without errors' or 'You're certainly getting on well with that task' through to more tangible rewards such as a certificate at the end of the course or a promotion at work.

Example

Jamie was sawing a piece of wood and hadn't paid attention to the health and safety regulations. The saw kept slipping and he cut his hand. His tutor gave him negative feedback and this, along with his cut, ensured he was always careful in future.

The training cycle

There are several theories regarding the training cycle. The chapters in this book will follow the format of identifying needs and planning, designing, facilitating, assessing and evaluating learning. The cycle can be followed by the tutor or by the student. It's called a cycle as you can start at any point, but you must follow through all the other points for training and learning to be effective.

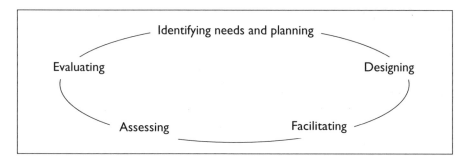

Your role as a tutor will usually follow the training cycle and involve the following.

- Identifying needs and planning – finding out the needs of the organisation and the students, preparing a scheme of work and session plans to deliver group or individual learning, based upon the needs of the organisation, the syllabus and the students.

- Designing – preparing the environment, suitable delivery resources and handouts.

- Facilitating – delivering teaching and learning in a suitable manner.

- Assessing – ensuring your students have learnt the necessary skills and knowledge.

- Evaluating – obtaining feedback from the students and evaluating yourself in order to modify or make changes in the future.

Example

You have been asked to deliver an existing course in flower arranging. This course was being delivered by someone who has now left. You have been given their scheme of work and session plans, handouts and presentations. You are therefore starting the cycle at the facilitating stage. You continue to deliver the course, assess your students and evaluate the whole process. Based upon this evaluation you revise the scheme of work, session plans, presentations and handouts ready for the next time.

Normally, you will plan the course yourself, based around the syllabus or the expectations of the organisation or students. You can then design your course materials before commencing your delivery or facilitation of the course. The word 'facilitation' is used as there are many different ways of delivering a subject, and students may learn for themselves as well as learning from their peers or you. You then assess your students to ensure they have acquired the necessary skills and knowledge. This is followed by an evaluation of the course and yourself in order to modify or change for the future.

Activity

Think about the subject you would like to deliver. What would you do in each stage of the cycle to ensure your delivery was effective? Would you follow all the stages?

It could be that you deliver a programme that your organisation has planned and prepared. They have set the programme and produced all the handouts. Therefore you are just facilitating the delivery of the subject. You may need to ask questions to assess learning but not evaluate the programme as the organisation will do this. Or you might be delivering a new course and have to carry out all the processes within the training cycle.

Learning styles

There is an old Chinese proverb:

I hear – I forget, I see – I remember, I do – I understand.

When you hear lots of information you may find it difficult to remember it all. If you can see something taking place that represents what you hear, you will remember more. However, if you actually carry out the task, you will understand the full process and remember how to do it again.

These are three different styles of learning, often referred to as aural, visual and kinaesthetic (Fleming 1987). Most people learn by a combination of more than one style.

Visual examples (seeing) – students usually:

- like to read and are often good spellers and have good handwriting;
- notice details;
- observe rather than act or talk;
- find verbal instructions difficult;
- are meticulous and neat in appearance.

Aural examples (listening and talking) – students usually:

- enjoy talking to others;
- like to try new things;
- hum, sing and whisper or talk out loud;
- are easily distracted;
- have difficulty with written instructions.

Kinaesthetic examples (doing) – students usually:

- like physical activities;
- fidget with pens whilst studying;
- like to try new things;
- do not like reading and are often poor spellers;
- use their hands whilst talking.

Visual, aural and kinaesthetic learning styles are often referred to as VAK. Not all students fall into one style; they may be multi-modal (i.e. a mixture of two or three styles). These types of student learn more easily than those with just one predominant style. It is therefore important to find out what learning style your students have, to enable you to deliver effective learning.

Activity

If you have access to the Internet, try a search for learning styles. You will find many different sites with free questionnaires for you to try out. You will receive an instant result. If you don't have Internet access, there are lots of books available, or your organisation may have examples.

One of the most widely used learning styles questionnaires is by Honey and Mumford (1986).

They suggest learners are a mixture of the following:

- activist;

- pragmatist;

- theorist;

- reflector.

Activist – students like to deal with new problems and experiences and like lots of activities to keep them busy. They love challenges and are enthusiastic.

Pragmatist – students like to apply what they have learned to practical situations. They like logical reasons for doing something.

Theorist – students need time to take in information, they prefer to read lots of material and think about something before applying it.

Reflective – students think deeply about what they are learning and the activities they could do to apply this learning. They like things that have been tried and tested.

Activity

Consider something you had to learn – for example, programming the video recorder for the first time.

Did you:

- **jump right in and press all the buttons (activist);**

- **look briefly at the instructions and then have a go (pragmatist);**

- **read the instructions, then think it through first (theorist);**

- **read the full manual and consider ways of doing it (reflective)?**

Knowing your students' learning styles will help you plan your sessions more effectively. However, what you may tend to do is deliver your sessions in the style in which you learn best – this will not help your students.

It is always useful to get your students to carry out a learning styles test. It can be fun and lead to a good discussion, as well as helping you plan your delivery methods based upon their learning styles.

Domains of learning

Learning goes through stages:

- attention;

- perception;

- understanding;

- short-/long-term memory;

- change in behaviour.

Bloom (1956) stated this can affect:

- thinking;

- emotions;

- actions.

These are called *domains*:

- cognitive;

- affective;

- psycho-motor.

When planning learning, you need to consider which domain you want to reach.

Example

If you are teaching historical facts, this would be the cognitive (thinking) domain.

If you are discussing the issue of fox hunting, this would be the affective (emotions) domain.

If you are demonstrating how to change a washer in a tap, this would be the psycho-motor (actions) domain.

You can use these domains when you are writing objectives for your students for example:

- students will quote specific dates and facts from the Second World War (cognitive/thinking);

- students will discuss their thoughts regarding environmental issues (affective/emotions);

- students will photocopy a document (psycho-motor/actions).

Motivation

Motivation is either *intrinsic* (from within), meaning the student wants to learn for their own fulfilment or *extrinsic* (from without), meaning there may be an external factor motivating the student, for example, a promotion at work.

Whatever level of motivation your students have will be transformed, for better or worse, by what happens during their learning experience with you. You therefore need to promote a professional relationship that leads to individual learning and trust. Some students may seem naturally enthusiastic about learning, but many need or expect you to inspire, challenge and stimulate them.

Many factors affect a student's motivation to work and to learn: interest in the subject matter, perception of its usefulness, a general desire to achieve, self confidence and self esteem, as well as patience and persistence.

To help motivate your students you need to:

- treat them with respect and as individuals;

- set clear targets;

- maintain an organised and orderly atmosphere;

- make tasks interesting, practical and relevant;

- vary your delivery styles to reach all learning styles;

- challenge and support those who need it;

- ask open questions;

- give ongoing constructive feedback;

- avoid creating intense competition;

- be aware of their attention span.

Maslow (1960) introduced a *hierarchy of needs*. These five needs represent different levels of motivation and have been adapted by other theorists as time has progressed.

The highest level was labelled *self actualisation*, meaning people are fully functional, possess a healthy personality, and take responsibility for themselves and their actions.

Maslow also believed that people should be able to move through these needs to the highest level provided they are given an education that promotes growth.

The following diagram shows the needs expressed as they might relate to learning.

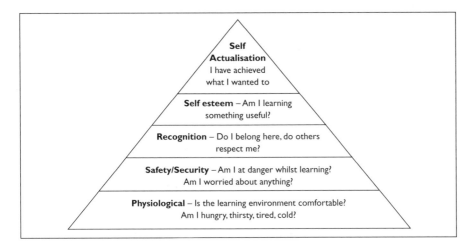

When we satisfy our needs at one level, we should progress to the next. Something may set us back a level, but we keep striving upwards. It is these needs that motivate us. However, some people may not want to progress through the levels, and may be quite content where they are at that moment in their life.

Always ensure that the learning environment you create meets your students' first-level needs. This will enable them to feel comfortable and secure enough to learn and progress to the higher levels. You will need to appreciate that some students may not have these lower needs met in their home lives, making it difficult for them to move on to the higher levels.

Activity

Think back to an environment where you learnt something new. Did anything hinder your learning? If so, what was it?

Perhaps the room was too hot or too cold, you were hungry, or you didn't receive any feedback or support from your tutor. All these can affect your learning and progression. As a tutor, you need to take all these factors into consideration when planning your delivery, whether one to one or in a group situation.

Most students respond positively to a well-organised course taught by an enthusiastic tutor who has a genuine interest in them and the subject.

Pedagogical and andragogical models of learning

A *pedagogical* approach is mainly tutor centred – the tutor does most of the talking and the students are usually passive. An *andragogical* approach places more emphasis on what the student is doing; they carry out tasks and learn new skills and knowledge for themselves. An andragogical approach is therefore mainly student centred.

In the pedagogic model, tutors assume responsibility for making decisions about the learning process. The tutor directs the learning; the student may not have any say, and their learning styles may not have been taken into consideration.

Knowles (1978) is the theorist who brought the concept of adult learning to the fore. He has argued that adulthood takes place when people behave in adult ways and believe themselves to be adults.

Most formal education still focuses on the tutor (pedagogy) rather than the student learning for themselves (andragogy). As a result, many students leave school having lost interest in learning. By adulthood, some people may have become apprehensive and not enjoy their learning. These experiences will therefore affect them.

Depending upon your subject, you may deliver in a pedagogical way, an andragogical way or a mixture of both.

Summary

In this chapter you have covered:

- Theories regarding principles of learning;
- The training cycle;
- Learning styles;
- Domains of learning;
- Motivation;
- Pedagogical and andragogical models of learning.

Theory focus

Books

Bloom BS (ed.) (1956) *Taxonomy of Educational Objectives, The Classification of Educational* Goals, McKay.

Daines JW et al (2002) *Adult Learning, Adult Teaching,* 3rd edition, Welsh Academic Press.

Knowler MS et al (2005) The adult learner: the definitive classic in adult education and human resource development, Butterworth-Heinemann.

Kolb DA (1984) *Experiential Learning: Experience as the Source of Learning and Development,* Prentice-Hall.

Laird D (1985) *Approaches to Training and Development,* Addison Wesley.

Rogers CR (1983) *Freedom to Learn for the 80s,* Merrill.

Skinner BF (1974) *About Behaviorism,* Knopf.

Websites

B F Skinner Foundation – bfskinner.org

Cognitive Learning Styles – http://tip.psychology.org/styles.html

Educational sites and resources – support4learning.org.uk

Educational theory – businessballs.com

Informal Education Encyclopedia – infed.org/encyclopaedia.htm

Honey and Mumford Learning Styles – peterhoney.com

Learning styles test – vark-learn.com

Maslow AH – maslow.com

Oxford Brookes University Teaching & Learning – brookes.ac.uk

3 IDENTIFYING NEEDS AND PLANNING LEARNING

Introduction

In this chapter you will cover the following points.

- Identifying needs;
- Product and process models of delivery;
- Individual learning;
- Group learning;
- Induction;
- Icebreakers;
- Aims and objectives;
- Schemes of work;
- Session plans.

There are activities and examples to help you reflect on the above which will assist your understanding of planning the learning process. Appendix 4 is a useful scheme of work pro-forma and Appendix 5 a session plan pro-forma which you may like to use to plan learning.

This chapter contributes towards the knowledge and skills required for the City & Guilds 7302 Certificate in Delivering Learning: An Introduction:

→ Unit 2 – Planning and preparing sessions

→ Unit 3 – Delivery of a micro-teaching session.

This chapter contributes towards the knowledge and skills required for the City & Guilds 7302 Diploma in Delivering Learning:

→ Unit 2 – Designing learning programmes

→ Unit 5 – Communication, delivery and managing disruption; micro-teaching

→ Unit 8 – Professional practice – teaching/training

→ Unit 9 – Professional practice – case study.

This chapter contributes towards the knowledge and understanding required for the National Vocational Qualification (NVQ) in Learning and Development Level 3:

→ L3 – Identify individual learning aims and programmes

→ L4 – Design learning programmes

→ L5 – Agree learning programmes with learners

→ L6 – Develop training sessions

→ L10 – Enable learning through presentations

→ L12 – Enable individual learning through coaching

→ L13 – Enable group learning

→ L15 – Support and advise individual learners.

This chapter contributes towards the knowledge and skills required for the International City & Guilds Certificate and Diploma in Teaching and Supporting Learners:

→ Unit 1 – Identifying learners' needs

→ Unit 2 – Plan and prepare learning

→ Unit 3 – Delivering learning.

Identifying needs

The starting point for planning your delivery is usually based upon the needs of the organisation, for example, their curriculum. External agencies such as awarding bodies will give approval for a qualification to be delivered. They will supply a syllabus or guide which will contain all the information you require for the delivery and assessment of your subject. Other considerations may include funding from external agencies, some courses are only offered if funding can be obtained. The requirements of local businesses and individual needs may lead to bespoke training courses. Some courses may be offered *in house*, for example, at a place of work, or cater to the needs of staff or students without leading to a formal qualification. Certificates of attendance may be given, or the course may be a *taster* that could lead on to a qualification if there was a demand.

Whatever your specialist subject, your organisation should supply you with a relevant syllabus or guide. If one is not available, you may need to develop your own course content based around the subject to be delivered.

You will need to identify the learning needs, styles, aspirations and potential of your students. What they expect to learn may not be what you expect them to learn. Getting the level right, and the amount of delivery and assessment you will carry out, will only come by experience and you may need to ask others for help and advice. Identifying your students' needs can take place during an interview or when they commence the course.

Product and process models of delivery

Different models of delivery will influence what you must, should and could deliver to your students.

The *product* model focuses upon the outcomes of a course; for example, students passing assignments to obtain certification. The tutor often just delivers what *must* and *should be* delivered in order for the student to pass.

Example

Samantha is taking driving lessons in order to pass the practical driving test. She has already passed the theory test and wants to take the minimum amount of lessons to save money. She therefore will not learn all the other important aspects of driving a car such as how to check the oil, change a tyre, etc. Therefore what could be delivered is missed out.

The *process* model focuses on the content of the course and other relevant knowledge and skills that *could* be learnt and applied.

Example

Kelly is taking a course in word processing. She is paying for the course herself and is prepared to continue until she feels competent. As she has never used a computer before, she is also going to learn keyboard skills and file-management skills. This will be in addition to the word-processing skills. She is therefore getting the benefit of what must and should be covered as well as what could be delivered.

The best delivery focuses upon the process and the product models but will depend upon how much time you have to deliver the course content.

Activity

Think back to your school days. Did you take an exam at the end of the year and revise by looking at previous exam papers (product model)? Did this model help you get where you are today? Or did it just get you what you wanted, for example, a certificate?

You will need to decide what is essential to be delivered (the *must*), what is important (the *should*), and what is helpful (the *could*).

Individual learning

You may deliver your subject on a one-to-one basis as opposed to groups of students. This could be a theory or a practical session, sometimes referred to as *coaching*. The way you plan, deliver and assess would be different for an individual's needs rather than a group's needs and you will be able to cater solely to their particular learning styles. You may have more time to devote to one student as you would not be catering for other students' needs at the same time.

You would need to agree an *individual learning or action plan* with your student, outlining what you are going to cover and how you will do this. This could be reviewed over the course of your delivery, to take into account any additional needs or changes in circumstances.

When delivering learning on a one-to-one basis, you would need to remain professional and not get too personal with your student. You also need to treat them with respect, taking into account any prior learning and setting realistic goals for them to achieve. Working on a one-to-one basis may sound like the ideal delivery, but if your student is not committed to their learning you will need to motivate them and keep your sessions interesting and stimulating.

On a one-to-one basis, students may behave differently from in a group. You may have to refer your student to another tutor if you feel you cannot effectively meet their learning needs.

Example

Dan was being disruptive during a group session in English. When his tutor talked to him about this after the session, he admitted he was not good with spelling and was being disruptive to hide this fact. His tutor offered to give him one-to-one sessions, which he agreed to. Dan behaved very well during these sessions, improving his spelling quite dramatically with individual attention.

Group learning

A group is a collection of individuals. Each individual student will have their own personality and may behave differently in a group from with another individual. Group dynamics can change, for example, when new students commence a course late or there are personality clashes. You will need to make new students welcome, perhaps *buddying* them with another student, or challenge behaviour and change seating positions if there is disruption. When delivering learning to groups, you should enable all individuals to play a part in their learning and you may have to complete individual learning plans to address different needs. It is useful to know that people take on different roles when in groups.

Example

Meena has set her group of eight students a task whereby they have to work together to reach a desired outcome. Each student naturally fell into a role: Rosie became the 'leader', reading through the task to the others and keeping them on track. Dave was the 'questioner', always asking questions and clarifying the task. Steve was the 'information giver', telling the others of his experiences that relate to the task. Ling was the 'joker', providing light relief and humour. Tom was the 'supporter', giving support to the others for their contribution and increasing their confidence. Hassan was the 'summariser', adding nothing new, but reflecting on progress; and Chris was the 'follower', not contributing anything new. Amy was the 'completer,' ensuring the task was finished.

Although the students took on different roles, they did achieve the task as their roles all complemented each other. If the group was made up of four leaders and four followers, the task might not get done, or take a lot longer.

It is important to recognise the fact that people play different roles, not only during group activities, but also in group learning. You may recognise yourself as one of the role players in a recent group situation you have been in. You might also realise you play different roles with different people, depending upon the situation.

Sometimes group work can get out of control. Knowing the roles various students play will enable you to mix the students into different groups. Always try to treat group members as individuals and use their names. This should help encourage their confidence and development. Make sure you ask questions of all students in the group on an individual basis as well as asking questions open to all.

If you have to move room or venue part-way through a course, this can upset the group dynamics as students have to find a new *comfort zone*.

Groups of people also go through stages when they meet. Tuckman (1965) states that group participants go through five stages:

1. forming;

2. storming;

3. norming;

4. performing;

5. adjourning (added in 1975).

Forming – This is the *getting to know you* and *what shall we do?* stage. Group members may be anxious and need to know the boundaries and code of conduct.

Storming – This is the *it can't be done* stage. It's where conflict can arise, rebellion against the leader can happen and disagreements may take place.

Norming – This is the *it can be done* stage. This is where group cohesion takes place and the norms are established. Mutual support is offered, views are exchanged and the group co-operates.

Performing – This is the *we are doing it* stage. Individuals feel safe enough to express opinions and there is energy and enthusiasm towards the task.

Adjourning – This is the *we will do it again* stage. The task is complete and the group separates. Members often leave the group with the desire to meet again or keep in touch.

Most groups will progress through the five stages; however, some may not go through all of them, or even jump backwards or forwards. This shows that groups take time to form and work together effectively, therefore you need to take this into account when planning your delivery.

Induction

When you begin delivering learning to a new group or an individual, there are certain points you need to cover with them. This is known as an *induction* and is usually an introduction to the organisation and course.

The best way to ensure you cover everything is to use a checklist and give your students a copy.

Activity

Imagine you are to begin delivering your subject to a group of 15 students next month. What information would you need to give them?

Your responses may have included:

- facilities of the organisation, e.g. toilets, catering, parking, smoking;
- a tour of the site;
- health and safety procedures;
- course and qualification details and dates;
- the expectations of the students and ground rules;
- break times;
- assessment details.

Your organisation may already have a checklist for you to follow. You will probably have to complete some paperwork with your students during the first session. Don't let this take over – your students will want to leave having learnt something interesting.

Icebreakers

An 'icebreaker' is usually carried out at the beginning of a course, to help the students get to know each other. Team-building exercises (relevant to the subject or not) can also be carried out during the course to energise students, perhaps after lunch or during an evening session. They also help retain attention, keep motivation high and help the group to work together.

Whichever way you use an icebreaker, it should be designed to be a fun and light-hearted activity to:

- break down barriers;
- encourage teamwork and inclusion;
- reduce apprehension and nervousness;
- establish trust;
- create a suitable learning environment;
- build confidence;
- enable people to talk confidently in front of others;
- reduce intimidation;
- help people to relax.

Activity

You have a new group of 12 students starting next week and know they have never met each other before. What sort of icebreaker would you do with them and why?

You might decide to get your students to introduce themselves in front of the others. However, this can be a bit intimidating if none of the students have met before. They may be so apprehensive about speaking in front of everyone for the first time that they don't listen to anything else being said. A way around this is to place the group into pairs and ask them to chat to each other for five minutes about their hobbies and interests. They may find they have something in common and create a bond. Talking in pairs whilst everyone else is busy chatting creates an atmosphere where they will hopefully relax. You can then ask each person to introduce the other person they have been chatting to. People may not feel comfortable talking about themselves to a group of strangers, so another person introducing them takes this anxiety away.

Your organisation may have icebreakers for you to use, or you can design your own or use existing ones.

Aims and objectives

These are educational terms used to express what you want your students to achieve and how you will go about this. The aim is the *what* and the objective is the *how*. Another term you may come across is *learning outcomes*, which is just another way of expressing objectives. Your aims and objectives will enable you to plan your delivery effectively, they are what you want your students to *know* and *do*.

Aim:

To provide students with the opportunity to acquire knowledge and understanding of the society in which they live.

Example objectives:

Students will list six different cultures of today's society.

Students will describe the characteristics of each culture listed.

The *aim* is the whole topic; the *objective* is the breakdown of that topic and what you want your students to achieve. Usually, the objective can be assessed or tested to check your students' learning.

Objectives should be SMART:

- Specific

- Measurable

- Achievable

- Realistic

- Time bound.

SMART objectives enable you to deliver and assess learning effectively.

SMART objective

Students will state the names of the Kings and Queens of England from 1066 to the present day.

This ensures that you can assess your students' knowledge and you would put a time limit on the activity. If you had used the objective: 'Know the Kings and Queens of England from 1066 to the present day', how would you know they know unless they named them as well? It's all about the way you word your objectives.

There are two types of objectives: *behavioural* and *non-behavioural*.

Behavioural – this is when the student can demonstrate their learning or be assessed upon it, e.g. 'the student will change a fuse in a plug'.

Non-behavioural – this is not specific and is more difficult to assess, e.g. 'to introduce the students to the law of gravity'.

Example words to use when writing SMART objectives are: 'demonstrate', 'describe', 'explain', 'list', 'perform' and 'state'.

This ensures they can be tested or assessed.

Words like 'know', 'understand' and 'discuss' are not SMART as they are more difficult to assess and are usually just people's opinions.

Activity

Think about the subject you would like to deliver, and write a suitable aim for your course (the 'what'). Break this aim down into a few objectives (the 'how').

Writing aims and objectives is a skill and will take practice. The more time you spend planning what you want your students to know and do, the more effective your delivery and their learning will be.

SMART words you could use when writing objectives are:

- analyse
- assemble
- calculate
- change
- clarify
- classify
- compare
- construct
- contrast
- convert
- create
- define
- demonstrate

- describe
- design
- estimate
- explain
- identify
- illustrate
- justify
- list
- maintain
- make
- measure
- operate
- organise

- perform
- practise
- present
- produce
- repeat
- review
- select
- show
- sketch
- state
- summarise
- use
- write.

General words you could use but which are more difficult to assess are:

- adopt
- allow
- apply
- appreciate
- assist
- develop
- discuss
- encourage
- establish
- evaluate
- explore

- familiarise
- help
- introduce
- justify
- know
- learn
- listen
- look
- manage
- outline
- plan

- prepare
- provide
- read
- recognise
- reflect
- relate
- see
- suggest
- teach
- understand
- watch

If you need to use any of the general words, try to use them in conjunction with a SMART word. Always make sure the words you are using are of the right level for your students, e.g. to list is easier than to evaluate.

Example

Students will look at and discuss in groups the latest government White Paper on education, listing and explaining the main points within 30 minutes.

Schemes of work

A scheme of work is prepared in advance of delivery to enable you to plan learning in a progressive way. It should take into account all the syllabus or course requirements and be broken down into sessions. Your scheme of work will broadly state what you will cover during each session; a more thorough form called a *session plan* will outline all the teaching and learning activities in detail, with allocated timings and assessment activities.

When planning your scheme of work, it is useful to know a bit about your students. This will enable you to take into account any special learning requirements and individual needs. A rationale will help you when planning and can include: who, what, when, where, why and how – five 'Ws' and one 'H' (WWWWWH). To help you remember, use the phrase When William Went Wrong What Happened?

A scheme of work should always include:

- who the sessions are for, the course title and aim (who and why);
- objectives or learning outcomes (what);
- duration and location of the sessions (when and where);
- activities, resources and assessment (how).

There is an example pro-forma available in Appendix 4. Your organisation may have a standard form for you to use or you may wish to design your own.

Things to consider when planning your scheme of work include:

- the syllabus – what has to be covered, remember *must*, *should* and *could*;
- how will you divide this into aims and objectives?
- in what order should they be delivered?
- how will sessions/time be allocated and linked?
- induction and initial assessment;
- your students – their age range, ability levels, differentiation, language, previous knowledge;
- resources, facilities and the environment;
- assessment – how you will do this.

Whether you are delivering on a one-to-one or group basis, it is important to have a scheme of work to follow. This can be modified as you progress through your delivery, but you need to plan in advance to ensure you are prepared for all your sessions.

Don't worry if you don't stick to your scheme of work because of changes – this is normal. It shows you are taking into consideration your students' needs.

Session plans

A session plan should be produced in advance of your delivery, and relate to your scheme of work. If you are just delivering a one-off training session, you won't need a scheme of work. For a one-to-one practical delivery you might use a *coaching plan*. This is similar to a session plan but is geared to one-to-one delivery rather than groups.

A session plan is more thorough than a scheme of work and includes details such as:

- tutor, date, time, room;
- aim of session;
- objectives of session;
- tutor activities and timing;
- student activities and timing;
- resources and how they will be used;
- assessment activities;
- self-evaluation.

The plan should also take into account different learning needs and styles.

To prepare your plans, you need to know details in advance about your students and the venue you will be using. An example pro-forma is available in Appendix 5. Your organisation may have a standard form for you to use or you may wish to design your own. Try not to prepare too many session plans in advance, as circumstances may change.

Each plan should have an introduction, development and conclusion; in other words, a beginning, middle and end. Your introduction should include the aim of the session and a recap of the previous one (if applicable). If this is your first session, make sure you introduce yourself, explain the facilities of the organisation and carry out an icebreaker. The development stage is the main delivery of your subject. Your conclusion should include a summary of your original aim. You can then state what the aim of your next session will be.

There should be a logical progression through these stages and your delivery should be in short but manageable chunks. Remember the Chinese proverb:

I hear – I forget, I see – I remember, I do – I understand.

You should always evaluate your session, either making notes as you progress or afterwards. You can note your strengths, areas for development and any action and improvements required for the future.

When planning a session, you need to consider your overall aim (the *what*) and break this down into objectives (the *how*). You can then allocate time to the various objectives. You also need to consider how you are going to assess your students, e.g. by questions or tests, and how you are going to recap their learning. Don't expect too much from your students, they don't know what you know. They need time to assimilate new knowledge and you will need to plan time for questions.

Be prepared – better to have too much than not enough. Unused material can be carried forward to another session or given as homework. Also, consider students who may finish tasks early, can you give them something else?

Activity

Watch one of the main news programmes on television. Notice how the presenters introduce the stories, then explain them in more detail and recap them at the end. Often there are two presenters, one male and one female, the camera shots change and there are videos and pictures to back up the stories. They will have planned and prepared well, having a contingency plan in case anything goes wrong. Did you take into account what the presenters look like and what they were wearing? Did this distract you in any way from the stories?

By watching the professionals deliver the news, you can learn how to apply their skills to your own delivery.

Summary

In this chapter you have covered:

- Identifying needs;
- Product and process models of delivery;
- Individual learning;
- Group learning;
- Induction;
- Icebreakers;
- Aims and objectives;
- Schemes of work;
- Session plans.

Theory focus

Books

Belbin M (1996) *Team Roles at Work*, Butterworth Heinemann.

Daines JW et al (2002) *Adult Learning, Adult Teaching*, 3rd edition, Welsh Academic Press.

Minton D (2005) *Teaching Skills in Further and Adult Education*, 3rd edition, Thomson Learning.

Websites

Tuckman, BW – coe.ohio-state.edu/btuckman

Icebreakers – http://adulted.about.com/cs/icebreakers/a/icebreakers.htm

4 DESIGNING LEARNING

Introduction

In this chapter you will cover the following points.

- Creating a suitable learning environment;
- Information communication technology;
- Resource materials;
- Delivery equipment.

There are activities and examples to help you reflect on the above which will assist your understanding of how to design learning.

This chapter contributes towards the knowledge and skills required for the City & Guilds 7302 Certificate in Delivering Learning: An Introduction:

→ Unit 3 – Planning and preparing sessions and delivery of a micro-teaching session.

This chapter contributes towards the knowledge and skills required for the City & Guilds 7302 Diploma in Delivering Learning:

→ Unit 3 – Designing learning resources

→ Unit 5 – Communication, delivery and managing disruption; micro-teaching

→ Unit 8 – Professional practice – teaching/training

→ Unit 9 – Professional practice – case study.

This chapter contributes towards the knowledge and understanding required for the National Vocational Qualification (NVQ) in Learning and Development Level 3:

→ L6 – Develop training sessions

→ L7 – Prepare and develop resources to support learning.

This chapter contributes towards the knowledge and skills required for the International City & Guilds Certificate and Diploma in Teaching and Supporting Learners:

→ Unit 2 – Plan and prepare learning

→ Unit 3 – Delivering learning.

Creating a suitable learning environment

A suitable learning environment is crucial to enable your students to learn effectively. This involves not only the venue and resources used, but your attitude and the support you give to your students.

You may be delivering learning in a college, the community, workplace, training room or other venue. You may be restricted by the availability of some resources, therefore you need to be imaginative with those you do have. Your students don't need to know if your organisation lacks resources. Your professionalism should enable you to deliver your subject successfully. However, you do need to take into account any health and safety issues and let your employer know if this will have an affect upon your students' learning.

Your students need to feel safe and comfortable in a positive and supportive environment. You need to ensure the venue is accessible to all and that facilities such as toilets and refreshment areas are suitable. If your session includes a break, make sure you tell your students what time this will be and for how long. Consider flexible breaks and individual needs. If you don't, students may not be concentrating on their learning but thinking about when they can get a drink or go to the toilet.

Students need to know why it is important for them to learn, what they are going to learn and how they will do this. Giving clear aims or targets is the starting point; summarising regularly, varying your delivery methods and taking learning styles into account will all help. Having a sense of humour and making learning fun will help your students remember key points. Your students need to believe that what they are learning has real value and meaning. You also need to treat each student as an individual and with respect, using their name wherever possible. You should always introduce yourself to your students. You could also write your name on the board or flipchart or wear a name badge.

Activity

Think about the subject you would like to deliver. What type of venue and resources would you like to use?

If you are teaching a practical subject, you would need a suitable room so that you can demonstrate and the students can practise. You may also need specialist equipment. Or you might not need a room; for example, if you are a driving instructor you would need a suitable vehicle.

If you are delivering a theoretical subject, you may be fine in a classroom but you might need a computer and projector for your presentations. You might be delivering a seminar in a venue you have never visited before. If this is the case, it would be useful to telephone or visit in advance to check what facilities are available.

You need to manage the learning environment so that it promotes and encourages individual and group learning. The seating arrangements can have a big impact on your students' learning. If you are working with groups, tables in rows do not allow people to interact well, if you can, move the tables to create smaller groups. A horseshoe layout will allow all your students to see each other and enable you to use eye contact with them all. People like their *comfort zones* and you may find that students will sit in the same place each time. This is often the place they sat at the first session. This is useful to help you remember their names as you can sketch a seating plan and write them down. Remembering their names will show respect, and encourage them to talk to you in confidence if they have any problems. Moving students around can either help or hinder their learning depending upon their maturity and the group dynamics.

Activity

Thinking about the subject you wish to deliver, consider the ways you feel the environment, e.g. type of room, layout of furniture, heating, lighting, etc., can impact upon your students' attitudes to learning. You may like to consider your own experiences as a learner.

Your responses may have included the size of the room: too big or too small. It might have been too hot, cold, light, dark or noisy. Whilst you may be very good at delivering your subject, you might have no control over the environment and will need to create a suitable atmosphere. Your enthusiasm and passion for your subject will help make your students' learning interesting. If you can also make it fun and varied, they will enjoy the experience and remember more about the subject and you, rather than the environment.

You may have to deal with unexpected situations. It is useful to have a contingency plan just in case.

Example

You are due to deliver a presentation to a group of 12 students at 7 pm. You have prepared transparencies for use with the overhead projector as there isn't a computer in the room. You have arrived at the venue half an hour early to prepare. You find there are tables that will seat six students comfortably, but only four chairs at each. You switch on the overhead projector and the bulb blows. If you didn't have a contingency plan you would not have been able to deliver the session. However, because you were early you were able to ask the caretaker to bring you four extra chairs and locate a spare bulb. You have also prepared handouts of your presentation to give your students which you can talk through if a replacement bulb cannot be found.

Preparing for unforeseen circumstances comes with experience. Whenever you are due to deliver a session, ask yourself: 'what would I do if something wasn't available?' You might prepare a computerised presentation to deliver, with handouts to give your students. However, if you can't get copies made in time, you can still deliver your presentation and offer to e-mail a copy to your students or get photocopies done later.

Some other issues you may encounter include:

● the room is untidy with rubbish on the floor, therefore you have to tidy it before you commence;

● there is writing on the board so you have to clean it;

● the overhead projector is missing – if another cannot be obtained, ensure there are enough handouts for all students and/or use other suitable media;

● the computer isn't connected to the projector for your presentation – this could simply be a loose cable connection which you can fix.

As a tutor, you need to take responsibility for ensuring the environment is suitable for your delivery and the students' learning. The following checklist will help:

● prepare your resources and presentations in advance;

● arrive early and set up the room according to your delivery methods and activities;

● ensure there is enough seating and workspace for all;

● have a contingency plan if anything goes wrong and act professionally in front of your students if it does;

● ensure the room is warm or ventilated, well lit, clean and tidy;

● write up your flipcharts/board neatly – check for errors;

● check any computerised equipment is working;

- check if you can use other rooms for breakout activities or group work;

- check what facilities are available, e.g. toilets, coffee machine, canteen, library, and let your students know where these are and when breaks will be;

- inform your students of the fire regulations and evacuation procedure;

- make sure you have a watch or small clock on your table so you can keep track of the timing of your delivery;

- take into account any special requirements of students, e.g. disabilities;

- leave the room tidy and secure when you finish, close windows and switch off all equipment;

- evaluate your session in order to modify or improve it for the future.

If you can develop the conditions for learning that are based on respect and trust and address the needs of individual students, you will have created a suitable learning environment.

Information communication technology

You may be required to use computerised equipment such as an *interactive whiteboard*. This is a recent innovation that has replaced the whiteboard. With a whiteboard, once you have written on it, you need to clean it before writing more material. With the interactive whiteboard, you use a special pen and the information is displayed on the board, and transferred to a computer for saving, printing and e-mailing. You can move between pages of text, link to the Internet and demonstrate tasks. If you are not very confident with your handwriting or spelling and grammar, you may need to practise.

Example

Angela is delivering a word-processing session and needs to demonstrate how to use the cut-and-paste tool. She can display the program on the interactive whiteboard and with the special pen, demonstrate to the group how to cut and paste. Previously, she would have had to gather the group around one small computer screen.

Other equipment you may use includes specialist software for delivering presentations. This would enable you to use graphics as well as text to make your presentation more visual. You can prepare your presentation in advance and save it to a disk or memory stick. Therefore as long as a computer and data projector are available, you can deliver in any room.

You may also use digital cameras or visual recording equipment with your students. You could record a practical task, enabling the students to see themselves later to inform their learning.

If you are using ICT for your delivery, remember to vary your delivery methods to reach the different learning styles of your students. You might need to undertake further training before using this type of technology.

You might like to carry out a search on the Internet for your subject, as there might be lots of information you could use.

Resource materials

Whatever resources you use, it is important to cover all your students' learning styles and meet the differing needs of your students and the learning process. You should always evaluate the effectiveness of any resources you use, to modify or change them for future use.

Depending upon your subject, you may need to create resources for your students. This could be a handout of useful information, an exercise, activity or worksheet or it could be a complex working model used to demonstrate a topic.

Resources should promote equality of opportunity, enable students to acquire new skills and knowledge and also increase their understanding of the subject.

People are also a resource; you could invite specialist speakers or other tutors to talk to your students.

Putting posters on the wall of the room will help to reinforce points. Students may not always look at them consciously, but subconsciously will glance at them, taking in the information.

You might have to acknowledge your organisation's resource constraints and make best use of what is available.

Example

Robert has a group of students who are struggling with number recognition. He has produced a practical task which will enable his students to gain further practice working with numbers. His students see this as a fun game; they can work together and learn through the process.

When designing resources, any individual needs should be taken into account, for example, dyslexia, hearing impairment, sight impairment or physical disabilities. You may need to produce handouts in a larger-sized font, or ensure there is plenty of *white space* surrounding the text. White space is blank space on the page. You also need to consider the location, cost, challenges and benefits of using certain resources. If you are using or adapting work with a copyright, you will need to check you are not in breach of this. Using pictures as well as text and not putting too much information on a handout will help learning.

Activity

What resources could you use to effectively deliver your subject? Would you have to make any yourself? Are there some already available you could use or adapt?

It could be that you have delivered your subject before and already have some resources that you just need to update. You might need to talk to other people who have delivered your subject to see what they have used.

The most common resources are handouts, books and the use of presentation equipment. Other resources you could use include video and audio tapes, games, books, the Internet, models and slide displays.

When planning the use of resources, it is useful to have a rationale. You could remember the five 'Ws' and one 'H' (WWWWWH) to help you.

Example

Who – *a group of 12 students aged 16–18; one has dyslexia, all have a mixture of visual, aural and kinaesthetic learning styles.*

What – *a handout to reinforce learning, including text and graphics.*

When – *during an evening class.*

Where – *training room 4.*

Why – *to backup a lecture and test knowledge.*

How – *after the short lecture, give the handout and talk through it with the students. The students can then answer the questions leading to a group discussion.*

Delivery equipment

You may be limited to the type of equipment available within your organisation or there may be other resources available you didn't know about. If you can, vary your use of the equipment to make your delivery more interesting.

Example

Sarah is delivering a course in catering to a group of 20 students. Today the students are having a theory session about the storage of food. Sarah has produced a handout to back up her talk, to give to the students at the end of the session (this ensures they will not fiddle with it during the session). She is using an interactive whiteboard to link to the Internet, enabling her to display relevant websites that the students can see. She also has a flipchart on which to write key words.

Using a variety of resources in an interesting and informative way will help your students learn. It will also ensure you cover their different learning styles.

Some hints regarding resources and equipment.

- Use visuals as well as text, and talk through all handouts you give, otherwise students tend to put them in their file and not look at them again.

- Don't try to cover too much information in one session, allow time for questions and summarising.

- Read presentations slower than you would normally hold a conversation, repeat important points and summarise regularly.

- If you have a great deal of boardwork, consider putting most of it on the board before the session and make a copy of it as a handout (you could cover it up with paper and then reveal it when necessary).

- Consider using an overhead projector or computer presentation rather than writing on the board.

- Don't talk whilst writing (unless you can contort your body so that you're more or less facing the students) – students don't hear most of your words when they're spoken to the board.

- Limit the amount of material you display, making text larger and bolder.

- Some students might not be able to see material written on the very bottom of the board or the bottom of a display screen.

- When using an overhead projector (OHP), move the transparency up as you speak through the points, and keep some material covered up – revealing it as you speak. When talking through the points, always face your students, either reading from the transparency or standing next to the screen.

- Always check your spelling, grammar and punctuation.

- Evaluate the effectiveness of the resources you have used, to improve them for the future.

Summary

In this chapter you have covered:

- Creating a suitable learning environment;

- Information communication technology;

- Resource materials;

- Delivery equipment.

Theory focus

Books

Reece I, Walker S (2003) *Teaching, Training and Learning*, 5th edition, Business Education Publishers Ltd.

Wallace S (2005) *Teaching and Supporting Learning in Further Education*, 2nd edition, Learning Matters Ltd.

Websites

Copyright regulations – opsi.gov.uk/si/si2003/20032498.htm

Disability Rights Commission – drc.gb.org

Equal Opportunities Commission – eoc.org.uk

Health and Safety Executive – hse.gov.uk

Learning and Skills Network – lsneducation.org.uk

National Learning Network – nln.ac.uk/materials

Introduction

In this chapter you will cover the following points.

- Formal/informal delivery;

- Teaching and learning activities;

- Managing behaviour and disruption;

- Communication skills;

- Listening skills;

- Mentoring and support;

- Micro-teaching;

- Observing others.

There are activities and examples to help you reflect on the above which will assist your understanding of how to facilitate learning. Appendix 2 contains a useful checklist which you may like to use for your delivery.

This chapter contributes towards the knowledge and skills required for the City & Guilds 7302 Certificate in Delivering Learning: An Introduction:

→ Unit 3 – Planning and delivery of a micro-teaching session.

This chapter contributes towards the knowledge and skills required for the City & Guilds 7302 Diploma in Delivering Learning:

→ Unit 5 – Communication, delivery and managing disruption: mircro-teaching

→ Unit 6 – Observation and evaluation of an experienced teacher/trainer

→ Unit 8 – Professional practice – teaching/training.

This chapter contributes towards the knowledge and understanding required for the National Vocational Qualification (NVQ) in Learning and Development Level 3:

→ L9 – Create a climate that promotes learning

→ L10 – Enable learning through presentations

→ L11 – Enable learning through demonstrations and instruction

→ L12 – Enable individual learning through coaching

→ L13 – Enable group learning

→ L14 – Support learners by mentoring in the workplace.

This chapter contributes towards the knowledge and skills required for the International City & Guilds Certificate and Diploma in Teaching and Supporting Learners:

→ Unit 3 – Delivering learning.

Formal/informal delivery

The subject you are delivering will determine whether your style of delivery could be formal, informal or a mixture of both. Formal delivery methods could be lectures, demonstrations and presentations. Informal could be discussions, group work and practical activities.

If you are delivering theory, this will usually be on a more formal basis, perhaps using a presentation package, a board and handouts. Even if your sessions are formal, try and include the students by asking questions to check their knowledge.

Practical subjects can be more informal and involve the students with their own planning and learning. You will probably set tasks for them to carry out, but will need to manage the session carefully to maintain control.

Your subject should never bore your students. You need to inspire your students and maintain their interest. If you are passionate about your subject, your enthusiasm will show through.

However you plan to deliver, you need confidence. To help your confidence, imagine you are an actor playing a lead role on the stage. Your students don't need to know anything about you, there is no need for you to reveal anything personal about yourself. If you become too personal with your students you may lose respect. If you are nervous, stand tall, breathe deeply and pause for a second or two. It might seem a long time to you, but it isn't. Focus your thoughts, relax and enjoy what you are doing. A little tip if nerves do take over is to place your tongue on the roof of your mouth, no one will notice and you should feel better.

Your first session should always include an icebreaker to help the students relax. You can then go onto *housekeeping*, information about the organisation's facilities, fire procedures, breaks, expectations, etc., and agree ground rules if necessary. You should then state the aim of the session.

As you deliver, allow time for questioning and recapping important points. If you feel you are overrunning, carry something over to the next session, or give it as homework.

If you are delivering a sequence of sessions, always recap the previous session before commencing delivery of the current session. When delivering, notice the reactions of students; you might have to change your pace of delivery or introduce something practical to energise them. When you end the session, summarise the content and explain what will be covered in the next session. Plan time at the end for student questions and clearing up; you don't want to be rushed. If you are setting any homework, be clear about your requirements and hand in dates.

Teaching and learning activities

Having prepared your scheme of work, session plans and resources, you can begin delivering. Depending upon your subject and whether you will deliver on a one-to-one or group basis, you will need to choose an appropriate method, or mixture of methods that will facilitate successful learning. Ideally, these should encourage creativity and enthusiasm, not discriminate in any way and promote independent learning which is suitable to the student's needs and capabilities. You will need to take into account the venue and availability of equipment and resources. Using a mixture of visual, aural and kinaesthetic methods of delivery will help reach all the learning styles of your students.

Example

If your subject is theoretical, e.g. history, you may deliver by lecturing and asking questions to check knowledge. However, you could make this more practical by introducing group discussions, role plays and reviewing historical writing.

The following list contains examples of teaching and learning activities. You may like to research these further and/or experiment with the different methods.

- activities
- assignments
- buzz groups
- case studies
- coaching
- debates

- demonstration
- dictation
- discussion
- distance learning
- drawing
- e-learning

- essays
- experiential
- games
- group work
- instruction
- lecture

- online learning
- open learning
- practical work
- presentations
- projects
- questions
- quizzes
- reading

- reports
- research
- role plays seminars
- simulation
- surveys
- technology based learning
- tests
- tutorials

- visits
- visiting speakers
- word shower/brain storm
- workshops.

Activity

Think about the subject you wish to deliver. Which of the methods would be suitable and why?

Whichever methods you use, these should be appropriate to the subject, level and individual or group. They should provide an environment that stimulates and promotes learning. When using activities, make sure you give very clear instructions and a time limit. If the activity is to be carried out in small groups, knowledge of your students will help you decide if they have the maturity to group themselves or whether you need to group them.

Managing behaviour and disruption

To get through a delivery session without any disruptions would be wonderful, but this very rarely happens. You might have a student who arrives late, an inquisitive student who always wants to know more, or just someone asking to leave the room to go to the toilet. Whatever the disruption might be, you need to handle this professionally to minimise any effect it might have on your delivery and the group's learning. Don't just ignore the behaviour, address it immediately. However, with experience you will realise that some things can be ignored.

Example

You are giving a presentation to a group of 15 students during an afternoon session. Three students in the group begin talking among themselves about what they did at the weekend. Rather than reprimand them, you decide to stop speaking altogether and use eye contact with them. They soon realise you are no longer speaking and are looking at them. Because you were silent, they stopped talking and paid attention to you again.

Usually, disruptions occur because people don't follow the ground rules; for example, their mobile phone rings, they decide to eat or drink or do something other than that which you have asked them to do. If this is the case, politely ask them to stop, remind them of the ground rules and how they are also disrupting their peers' learning. Other occurrences happen because people are bored, they don't understand what you are saying or you are not challenging them enough. You could give them an alternative activity, get them involved with other students or have a quick one-to-one chat to help them.

Your students will be attending your course for different reasons. They may not be attending voluntarily, or they may be attending for social reasons rather than an interest in achieving a qualification. They may therefore not be as keen as you would like them to be and you will need to keep them interested and motivated.

Example

You are delivering a 12-week course of evening classes leading to a qualification in painting and drawing. There are 14 students in the group aged 20–65. The four older ones have told you they are only there because they always do something together and it gets them out of the house one evening a week. They are not interested in taking the qualification and often disrupt the group by digressing onto other topics. You motivate them by giving them a sense of personal achievement by aiming for the qualification. You also tell them that their life experiences could be used to help the younger students. When they digress, you encourage them to relate it to the subject and involve the entire group.

Ultimately, you need to find your own way of dealing with situations based upon your experiences. Don't show favouritism, lose your temper, make threats or touch students inappropriately. Try to have a positive approach, be firm, fair and friendly, be organised and structured with your delivery and keep a check on the time. Maintain motivation by including all students in their learning, keeping your sessions active wherever possible and deliver your subject in an interesting and challenging way.

Communication skills

Communication is a means of passing on information from one person to another. It is also a manner of expression, for example, your body language, voice and the gestures you make.

At the first meeting, your students will probably make a subconscious judgement about you, and you will probably make one of them. These judgements often turn out to be wrong; therefore it is important not to make any assumptions about your students.

Body language includes facial expressions, eye contact, gestures, posture, non-verbal signals and appearance. Your personality will show through when you are delivering learning. Some aspects you might not be able to control, such as facial flushing, blinking or clearing your throat. However, some you can control, such as winking, giving a thumbs-up sign or laughing. Some things you may not even realise you do, such as making gestures with your hands, and that is where it is useful to have a visual recording made of your delivery. If you need to write on a board or flipchart whilst speaking to your students, don't do both at the same time. If you face the board, they may not hear you speak and you might miss something happening in the room.

You not only need to be aware of your own body language, but that of your students. You need to sense what they are not saying as well as what they are.

Example

You are explaining a complex topic and notice one of your students is making a strange expression, furrowing his brow as if he doesn't understand. As you regularly use eye contact with all your students, you quickly spot this and ask them if they would like you to explain the topic again. You rephrase what you have just explained and see from their smiling and nodding face that they have understood. To double-check their learning, you ask an open question which requires an answer other than yes or no.

The language you use should reflect equality and inclusiveness, be relevant to the subject and not offend anyone in any way. You may have to practise with your voice projection, to ensure all students can hear you, but don't shout, just speak louder than normal and ask if students at the back can hear.

If you are knowledgeable about your subject, your confidence and enthusiasm will show through and you will give a professional delivery. Don't expect your students to remember everything first time; they don't know what you know. You should repeat or rephrase key points regularly. You might even get frustrated if asked questions regarding points you have already explained. Try not to say things like 'I just told you that' or 'Can't you remember what I just said?' Repeating key points will help your students remember them. Don't embarrass a student in front of their peer group; they may feel they can't ask you anything again.

Activity

Read the following list of words once, and then write down as quickly as you can the words you remember.

cat	deck	table	snow	storm
sky	plant	book	smile	sky
lulu	lala	sky	music	plant
tree	bottle	money	cat	plant

Among your words are probably: cat, plant, sky, lulu and lala. This is because they occur at the beginning, the end, are unusual or repeated words. Ensuring you state your aim clearly at the beginning of your session, recapping regularly and summarising at the end will help learning take place. However, don't introduce anything new in your summary as this will confuse your students. If you can make your session a little bit different, perhaps by introducing fun and laughter into your delivery, whilst remaining professional, this will also help learning take place.

The attention spans of individuals are all different, people need time to assimilate new knowledge and you will need to cater for this with your delivery and activities.

Learning occurs best in an active, not a passive environment. Welcome your students to the session; smiling will help them feel at ease. Try to get your students to take part in their own learning, move them and yourself around the room if appropriate. Always recap key points and ask open questions to check knowledge.

Listening skills

Effective listening only takes place when the person who receives the information interprets and understands it the way the deliverer intended.

It can be easy to say something and think you said it in a way that your student will understand, only to find them asking you to say it again or to rephrase it.

You can become a better listener by:

- not interrupting;

- using eye contact;

- watching body language – yours and theirs;

- leaving your emotions, arguments and thoughts behind;

- getting rid of distractions;

- avoiding reaching conclusions or hasty judgements;

- avoiding jumping in with questions or statements;

- listening for a key word which will help you clarify what is being said.

Listening skills don't just apply to you listening to your students but to them listening to you too.

To help your students hear you effectively, you should:

- speak clearly and slightly slower than normal;

- not complicate your speech by including too much too soon or using jargon and acronyms;

- not lose the point of what you are trying to put across;

- remain focused;

- ask questions regularly to check the student is listening.

Activity

Think about the last time you heard something important. This might have been some information from a colleague or friend/family member or perhaps you just listened to the news on the television or radio. Did you really hear what was being said, or did you just tune into the parts that interested you? Was your mind wandering elsewhere or were you distracted by something?

It is important to listen to your students, also, to hear what they are not saying by observing their body language.

Activity

Look at the following sentences from students and decide upon a suitable response, watch out for a key word to help you.

- *I'm sorry I'm late; I've got problems at home.*

- *I don't think I can do this assignment, it's too hard.*

- *You explain the topics well but go too fast for me to take it all in.*

The first key word is *problems*. You might like to ask the student if there is anyone that can help to ensure they arrive on time in future.

The second is *hard*. You could ask the student why they are finding it hard, perhaps you could break the assignment down into smaller parts to help them.

The third is *fast*. If this student feels this way, maybe others do too; you could then speak a little slower next time.

Mentoring and support

Giving the right support to your students is crucial to their learning and development. You may have identified a particular individual's needs during their initial assessment, or this may naturally occur during the learning process. Whichever way this is identified, you need to establish an effective support strategy and have access to appropriate sources of guidance. A mentor is a person who acts as a role model to guide and support someone through a learning and development process. You may be required to mentor a particular student or colleague. You might even have a mentor supporting you as you progress through your own learning.

Whether you are acting as a mentor, or just giving support, you need to create an environment which enhances access and participation throughout the learning programme. You will also need to explore potential areas of bias or prejudices in terms of your awareness of other people's cultures, religions, social identities, genders and sexuality. It is important not to impose your own values onto others, but to listen and respect theirs. You also need to know your own limit of expertise and when to refer them to someone else.

As a tutor, your students' needs can vary widely. This can range from guidance with assignment writing, study skills, support with numeracy, literacy, information technology to any special individual requirements such as support with dyslexia. You may not be a specialist yourself in any of these areas, but you will need to know how to access appropriate sources of guidance.

You may find your own skills developing further, for example communication, listening, mentoring, empathy and feedback. You may also wish to take further training to effectively support your students.

Support not only comes from people, but from resources as well. You may need to adapt or obtain specialist equipment to help your students.

You will also need to be aware of any health issues such as a student needing privacy to take insulin at a required time.

Don't ever feel you have to deal with everything yourself; always ask your organisation for help and guidance.

Example

You have a student who repeatedly arrives late. This disrupts the session and means she misses valuable information. You decide to chat to her at the end of the session and find out that the time of the bus service she usually uses has been changed. You know some of the group have their own vehicles and offer to ask if anyone could give her a lift. This was subsequently arranged and the student now arrives on time.

The types of support you offer to help your students may not always be this easy and you may have to refer to other people within your organisation or external agencies.

Micro-teaching

Think of this as a trial run of your delivery. You may be taking a Level 3 course at the moment and have to prepare and deliver a session to your peers. Your tutor might make a visual recording of this, enabling you to see things you didn't think you did. For example, you might twiddle with a ring or fiddle with coins in your pocket. You might also have to deal with disruptive situations from your students and need to remain professional throughout. It's a practical way of learning from your experience.

If you are not taking a course at the moment, it is always useful to practise your delivery on friends, family or colleagues. This helps you plan your timings, check your resources and will help build your confidence.

Think of it as a dress rehearsal: things will go wrong and it's okay to make mistakes as you will learn from them. Your peers will also give you valuable feedback which will help you evaluate your delivery and make modifications or improvements for the future.

You will need to prepare a session plan, arrive early to set up and check equipment and have plenty of resources available, e.g. handouts. Any visual materials you use should be checked for spelling, grammar and punctuation and not contain too much information or jargon. Have some open questions planned in advance and make sure you involve the entire group, using their names where possible.

Introduce yourself, your subject and your aim, try to put all individuals at ease and give encouragement and praise regularly. Encourage an atmosphere of trust and honesty. Speak clearly and a little slower than normal, and listen to what the participants ask or say, ensuring you follow up things you don't know. Use eye contact and if you move around the room to talk to individuals, come down to their eye level, don't stand over them. You might have to vary your tone, manner and pace of delivery depending upon the reactions of your participants. Recap key points regularly and summarise at the end. Try to relax, remain in control, confident and focused and above all enjoy yourself. You can then evaluate your delivery afterwards.

Appendix 2 contains a useful checklist for your delivery and micro-teaching sessions.

Observing others

It is always useful to observe an experienced practitioner, preferably in your own specialist subject. You might also learn a few things that you hadn't considered for the delivery of your own subject. You would need to ask their permission and arrange a suitable date and time.

Prior to your observation, it is useful to make a checklist of what you would be looking for.

Activity

You have arranged to observe one of your colleagues for an hour's session next Thursday at 6 pm. You aim to arrive early and will sit at the back of the room. What would you look for as part of your observation?

You would need to see their session plan, that it had clear aims and objectives with realistic times for delivery. The plan should also take into account individual needs and cater to all learning styles. You would also want to see how they set up the room and checked any equipment, taking into account health and safety and equal opportunities.

You would observe how the tutor created a rapport, delivered their introduction, recapped key points and asked questions, altering their pace or activities to suit the needs of the learners as the session progressed.

You would look at the types of resources and activities used, to ensure they where relevant to the students.

At the end of the session, you would observe how the tutor summarised the topics and explained the next session (if applicable) and then tidied the room.

After you have carried out the observation, you might like to give feedback to the tutor. It is always useful to reflect upon what you have learnt from the observation that you could use for your own delivery.

Summary

In this chapter you have covered:

- Formal/informal delivery;

- Teaching and learning activities;

- Managing behaviour and disruption;

- Communication skills;

- Listening skills;

- Mentoring and support;

- Micro-teaching;

- Observing others.

Theory focus

Books

Cowley S (2002) *Getting the Buggers to Behave*, Continuum International Publishing Group.

Daines JW et al (2002) *Adult learning, Adult Teaching*, 3rd edition, Welsh Academic Press.

Gelb MJ (1988) *Present Yourself*, Jalman.

Wallace S (2002) *Managing Behaviour and Motivating Students in Further Education*, Learning Matters Ltd.

Wallace S, Gravells J (2005) *Mentoring in Further Education*, Learning Matters Ltd.

Websites

Disability Government Site – direct.gov.uk

Disability Rights Commission – drc.gb.org

Educational Activities – businessballs.com

Encyclopedia of Informal Learning – infed.org

English and Maths online testing – move-on.org.uk

Equal Opportunities Commission – eoc.org.uk

Health and Safety Executive – hse.gov.uk

Icebreakers – http://adulted.about.com/cs/icebreakers/a/icebreakers.htm

National Programme for Specialists of Behaviour and Attendance – teachernet.gov.uk/wholeschool/behaviour/npsl_ba/

Introduction

In this chapter you will cover the following points.

- What is assessment?
- Why assess?
- Initial assessment;
- Independent assessment;
- Formative/summative assessment;
- Planning assessment;
- Methods of assessment;
- Validity and reliability;
- Questioning techniques;
- Making assessment decisions;
- Giving feedback;
- Reviewing progress;
- Keeping records;
- Standardisation;
- Quality assurance.

There are activities and examples to help you reflect on the above which will assist your understanding of the assessment process.

This chapter contributes towards the knowledge and skills required for the City & Guilds 7302 Certificate in Delivering Learning: An Introduction:

→ Unit 3 – Planning and delivery of a micro-teaching session.

This chapter contributes towards the knowledge and skills required for the City & Guilds 7302 Diploma in Delivering Learning:

(→) Unit 4 – Designing assessment activities

(→) Unit 5 – Communication, delivery and managing disruption: micro-teaching.

This chapter contributes towards the knowledge and understanding required for the National Vocational Qualification (NVQ) in Learning and Development Level 3:

(→) A1 – Assess candidates using a range of methods

(→) A2 – Assess candidates' performance through observation

(→) L3 – Identify individual learning aims and programmes

(→) L16 – Review progress with learners

(→) L20 – Support competence achieved in the workplace.

This chapter contributes towards the knowledge and skills required for the International City & Guilds Certificate and Diploma in Teaching and Supporting Learners:

(→) Unit 1 – Identifying learners' needs

(→) Unit 4 – Assess outcomes.

What is assessment?

Assessment is a way of finding out if learning has taken place. It enables you, the assessor, to ascertain if your student has gained the required skills and knowledge needed at a given point towards a course or qualification.

Why assess?

Learning can affect a person's knowledge, skills or attitudes. Depending upon the subject you are delivering you will need to devise different ways of assessing your students, to check their progress. You may also need to liaise with others who may be involved with the assessment and progress of your student, for example, at their place of work if they are employed or on work experience. You need to make a decision as to whether your students are competent or capable of passing a particular aspect of a course/qualification. Confirming this will enable them to progress further and/or obtain a qualification.

Activity

Think back to a course or qualification you have taken in the past. How do you remember being assessed? Consider:

- **Were you assessed during or at the end of the course?**

- **How did your tutor/trainer assess you?**

- **Did this assess your knowledge, skills or attitudes (or a mixture)?**

If your responses relate to experiences at school or college, you may have taken an examination at the end of the course, or completed assignments during the course. You may have had examination nerves and failed because of this, not because you didn't know your subject. If you had been assessed in a different way, you might have passed.

You may have attended an evening class to learn a foreign language. This would involve lots of conversations and questions, perhaps even a written test as well.

A course such as pottery or motor vehicle maintenance would have involved lots of practical tasks to enable you to demonstrate your skills, backed up with questions to check your knowledge.

Your last experience may have been your driving test. This would be a practical test to assess your skills as a driver, with a theory test to check your knowledge.

Planning assessment

Assessment is often carried out on an individual basis and should be written down and agreed with your student. Assessment may take place in the learning environment or the workplace.

When planning assessment, consider: who, what, when, where, why and how (WWWWWH). If you are designing a test, you need to make sure you write your questions very clearly and only test the relevant standards/learning outcomes. You also need to know what you are looking for and what answers you expect, it helps to have these written down before marking.

You also need to take into account equality of opportunity when deciding which assessment methods to use. You don't have to change the assessment criteria, just the methods you would use or the environment in which you would assess. You need to make sure you are not discriminating in any way and are supporting any students who may have additional needs. All students are entitled to a fair assessment and should be given the best opportunity to demonstrate their ability.

Assessment planning should be specific, measurable, achievable, realistic and time bound (SMART):

- Specific – the task relates only to the standards/learning outcomes being assessed and is clearly stated.

- Measurable – the task can be measured against the standards/learning outcomes, allowing gaps to be identified.

- Achievable – the task can be achieved at the right level.

- Realistic – the task is relevant and will give consistent results.

- Time bound – target dates are agreed.

Methods of assessment

There are several different ways of assessing learning and you need to decide which is best for your students. If you are delivering a course with a syllabus, this will usually tell you which methods to follow. This may be by assignments or tests. If you are assessing an NVQ, this will probably be in the workplace and you may need to liaise with other people to ensure you will not be disturbed and can visit on a certain day and time.

Assessments are usually:

- internal – produced by you or the organisation, e.g. questions, projects or assignments;

- external – set by an awarding body, e.g. an examination.

Whichever methods you choose, you need to treat each student as an individual as their needs may be different.

Example

If you have a dyslexic student it may be appropriate to set additional course work in place of a formal test. For a partially sighted student you could give papers in a larger font or give additional time for them to read the questions and check their answers. For a deaf student, you could give a written test instead of an oral test. For some students who might struggle with spelling and grammar, the use of a computer or a tape recorder could help.

The following, in no particular order, are some methods of assessment you could use depending upon your course/qualification and should all be adapted to suit individual needs.

Observation

Watching students perform a skill lets you see just how well they are doing. Let your student make a mistake (if it is safe) rather than interrupt them. You can then ask questions later to see if they realised. You can also observe group work and presentations; this can encourage students to comment upon each other. As an assessor, you would need to make a decision as to the contribution of each student if it was part of a group exercise.

Questions (written or oral)

Questions can be used to assess knowledge and understanding. Be careful if you are using the same questions for different students as they may pass on the answers. You may need to rephrase some questions if your students are struggling with an answer. Poor answers are often the result of poor questions. For essay and short answer tests, write out sample answers. These will give you something against which to compare your students' answers. Be careful with the use of jargon – just because you understand it doesn't mean your students will.

If you are asking questions verbally to a group of students, ensure you include all students. Don't just let the keen students always answer first as this gives the ones who don't know the answers the chance to stay quiet. Ask a question, pause for a second and then give the name of a student who can answer. This way, all students are thinking about the answer as soon as you have posed the question, and are ready to speak if their name is asked. When asking questions, only use one question in a sentence, as more than one may confuse your students. Try not to end a session with 'do you have any questions?' because often only those that are keen or confident will ask, and this doesn't tell you what the students have learnt. Try not to use questions such as 'does that make sense?' or 'do you understand?', as your students will often say yes as they feel that's what you expect to hear. It doesn't tell you whether they have learnt or not.

Professional discussion

This is a method by which you will have a conversation with your student based around the standards/learning outcomes of the course/qualification. You will need to be careful how you word your questions and sentences, to be able to ascertain the responses you need. You will also need to keep a note of what was discussed, and/or tape record the discussion. Professional discussions are useful to fill any gaps not demonstrated by the student.

Past experience and achievements

This involves noting what has previously taken place to find a suitable starting point for further assessment. It may be that a student has started a course elsewhere and then transferred to you with some work already completed. This is often referred to as accreditation of prior experience/learning (APEL).

Tests

Tests can include multiple-choice questions to check knowledge. You will need a marking scheme for any tests you carry out. Be careful how you administer these tests. You need to ensure that students have not seen each other's answers in case you use the same tests for different students at different times.

Assignments, activities, projects, tasks and/or case studies

These could assess several areas of learning over time. A well-written project will help the student provide evidence of knowledge and skills. This is often known as *holistic* assessment as it assesses several aspects of a course/qualification. If you are using a scheme of work, you will need to carefully plan the dates of issue and return. This will help with your own timing for marking and feedback and ensuring the work is equally distributed throughout the course. Some assignments are set by the awarding body and will have clear marking criteria for you to follow.

Simulations

These are used when it is not possible to carry out a task, perhaps to assess whether students can successfully evacuate the building in case of a fire. You don't need to set fire to the building to observe this process.

Written reports

These reports are a form of self-assessment. You may not have the opportunity to see the student perform, for example they may be carrying out tasks at work. They could write a report and back this up with statements from colleagues. The student will need to be specific about what they have achieved and what they need to do to complete any gaps.

Evidence from others

This is often referred to as a witness testimony. Other people may be involved with the student's progress, they can write a statement to show how the student has successfully covered relevant aspects of the course/qualification. You would always need to check the authenticity of any witnesses used.

Learning journals

These are useful methods of ascertaining if a student has put theory into practice. They will also confirm to you the writing skills of your students. If learning journals are used to make an assessment decision, it is beneficial to encourage the student to cross-reference their writing to the standards/learning outcomes.

Portfolios

These are often used by students working towards NVQs and may contain records of observations and questions, along with witness testimonies and product evidence. Product evidence is based around the work the student has carried out and may include letters, memos, forms, etc. (as long as they remain confidential). You then decide if all the evidence successfully covered the standards/learning outcomes. Some portfolios are now produced electronically and saved to a website or CD-ROM. You would need to access this data to make a decision. You also need to make sure your student completed the work themselves and they may have to sign an authenticity statement.

Electronic assessment

Modern technology enables assessments to be taken online. These could be marked automatically by a specialist computer program, enabling instant results. Electronic assessments could be carried out in the training centre, student's home or a library. The authenticity of the work would have to be carefully monitored.

Activity

Look at the following list. Which assessment method/s could you use for each?

- **Changing a fuse**
- **Testing historical dates**
- **Answering the telephone**
- **Understanding geographical facts**
- **Evacuation of a building**
- **Cake decorating**
- **Bandaging limbs**
- **Spelling and grammar.**

You may have realised that observation and questioning can be used for most of them. These are the most commonly used methods of assessment for courses that do not involve an examination.

Validity and reliability

All assessment methods should be *valid*, i.e. assess what is meant to be assessed, for example only the relevant criteria in the syllabus or course guide.

Example

If you are going to assess word processing, you would not ask questions about spreadsheets.

Assessments should also be *reliable* – if the assessment was done again with a similar group/student, would you receive similar results? You may have to deliver the same subject to different groups of students at different times. If other assessors are also assessing the same course/qualification as you, you need to ensure you are all making the same decisions.

Activity

Think again of an assessment you have taken. Did you feel it was valid and reliable?

If you could, would you have changed anything about the way you were assessed?

Your responses may reveal that you were quite happy with the way you were assessed because you didn't know any different at the time. Or you may have felt the assessment methods used were not really effective for you and you didn't enjoy the subject because of this.

If you are going to assess your own students, you need to know what you are to assess and then decide how to do this. The *what* will come from the standards/learning outcomes of the course/qualification you are delivering. The *how* may already be decided for you if it is assignments, tests or examinations.

You need to consider the best way to assess the skills, knowledge and attitudes of your students, whether this will be formative and/or summative and how the assessment will be valid and reliable.

All work assessed should be valid, authentic, current, sufficient and reliable, this is often known as VACSR – try to remember the phrase 'Valid Assessments Create Standard Results'.

- Valid – the work is relevant to the standards/criteria being assessed.

- Authentic – the work has been produced solely by the student.

- Current – the work is still relevant at the time of assessment.

- Sufficient – the work covers all the standards/criteria.

- Reliable – the work is consistent across all students, over time and at the required level.

Questioning techniques

It is always useful to ask questions to check your students understand why they are doing a task. Try to use *open* questions. These are questions that do not expect a yes/no answer and usually begin with:

who; what; when; where; why; how.

Example

'Why did you decide to put those items in that order?' The response would have to be stated, it cannot be a simple yes or no, and therefore demonstrates understanding.

Yes or no responses are from *closed* questions and can be useful for facts.

Questions are not really useful for assessing skills, but can inform you if your stu-

Example

'Did the battle of Hastings take place in 1066?' The answer would be yes, but this doesn't tell you if the student understands why it took place in 1066. To find out more, you could follow the closed question with an open question such as 'Why did it take place in that year?'

dent has the knowledge to back up their skills.

If you have to write your own questions for students, think how you will do this e.g. short questions, long questions (essay style, e.g. 1000 words), open, closed, multiple choice or an assignment. Will you be grading, e.g. A, B, C, or just passing/referring? Whichever method you use, you need to be clear with your questions and only assess what is necessary, keeping it valid and reliable. A pass would show the student has covered everything expected, a refer would show the student needs to do some more work.

If you are grading, you will need to follow clear criteria as to how you reach your decision, so that you are being fair to all students. You may have to write these criteria yourself or it may form part of the guidance that comes with the syllabus.

It's important not to make the questions too complex, therefore don't ask two or more questions in one sentence. Always check your spelling, grammar and punctuation and be careful with the use of jargon and acronyms.

Multiple-choice questions should have a clear question and three or four possible answers. The question is known as the *stem*, the answer is called the *key* and the wrong answers are called *distracters*. Answers should always be similar in length and complexity. Answers should not be confusing, and there should only be one definite key.

Example

To forward an e-mail you would:

A produce a hand draft first

B check all spelling and grammar

C only need the sender's address

D retain all the original content

You will see that all the answers contain five words and are similar in length. None of the answers contains a clue from the question. A, B and C are the distracters and D is the correct answer (the key).

Activity

Have a go at writing the following questions:

● *a closed question based around your own subject (with a possible answer);*

● *an open question based around your own subject (with a possible answer);*

● *a multiple-choice question based around your own subject, with three distracters and one answer key (keep a note of the correct answer).*

You may have found it easy to write the closed question as this has a firm answer, but the open question could gain different responses if not carefully phrased. The multiple-choice questions would have been harder to write as the distracters and key need to be very similar, but one must be the clear answer and not include any clues from the question.

Making assessment decisions

Depending upon the course/qualification you are assessing, there will be different guidelines as to what will constitute a pass, refer or fail. If you are assessing a competence-based course, e.g. an NVQ, students are either competent or not yet competent. When making a decision, you need to remain objective and only assess what you are meant to assess and nothing else. You could make a decision which your student might complain or appeal against; you need to find out the procedures for the organisation in which you work just in case.

Activity

Think back to the last time you received feedback from someone for something you did. This might not have been in a learning situation, perhaps it was something you did for a family member at home, for a colleague at work, or for a friend. Was this feedback positive? Did it leave you feeling motivated and good about what you had done? Or did it leave you feeling demotivated and not willing to try again?

Giving feedback

Whichever way you decide to assess your students, you need to give feedback at a suitable time and place. Feedback should be more thorough than just a comment. It shouldn't be your opinion, but facts that relate to success or otherwise. If you have any students with learning difficulties, feedback should be adapted to their level of understanding and given in a way which will encourage their development.

Feedback is usually given on a one-to-one basis after assessment takes place. If group feedback is given for a task they have all worked towards, try to give each person an individual comment about their contribution, and then state clearly whether the task was achieved, or if not, why not.

If you are marking questions, the feedback might be written down and handed to the students at a later date. Try to avoid using words like *excellent* or *satisfactory* as these don't really help the student know why it was excellent or just satisfactory. If you like to use the word *excellent*, expand your feedback to say why it was excellent.

You should give your students a deadline by which to submit their work, and then let them know when they will receive feedback. You could give verbal feedback and/or written feedback.

Always encourage your students to ask questions and be positive when stating areas for development.

Constructive feedback doesn't just mean positive feedback. Negative feedback, if given carefully, can be very important and useful to the student. Be specific about what could be improved and always state why.

Most people need encouragement, to be told when they are doing something well and why. When giving feedback it can really help the student to hear first what they have done well, followed by what they need to improve, and then end on a positive note or question to keep them motivated.

Example

'The layout of the table is fine, knives, forks and spoons are in the correct places; however, the napkins are a bit creased. What could you do to put that right?'

Usually, the focus of feedback is likely to be on mistakes rather than strengths. If the positive is stated first, any negative comments are more likely to be listened to and acted upon. Starting with a negative point may discourage your student from listening to anything else that is said and demotivate them.

Try to avoid general comments that are not very useful when it comes to developing skills. Statements such as 'You were brilliant' or 'That was awful' may be pleasant or dreadful to hear, but they do not give enough detail to develop learning. Try to pinpoint what the person did which led you to use the word brilliant or awful.

Example

Positive: 'That was brilliant, the way you asked that question just at that moment was really helpful.' Or negative: 'That was awful, at that moment you seemed to be imposing your values on others.'

If you do offer negative feedback then don't simply criticise but suggest what the student could have done differently. Turn the negative into a positive.

Example

'The fact that you remained seated when Aisha came in gave an unwelcoming impression. I think if you had walked over and greeted her it would have helped put her at ease.'

It is important to take responsibility for the feedback you give. Beginning the feedback with 'I' or 'In my opinion', is a way of taking ownership of the feedback. Starting the feedback with 'I' rather than 'you' is more helpful.

Example

'I felt you did that really well as all the items were put in the correct order,' rather than 'You didn't get the items in the correct order.'

Sometimes, when giving feedback, you may start with something positive and then need to go onto something negative. Often, the word *but* is used; using the word *however* is much easier for the student to accept.

Example

'I felt your comments were very useful; however, if you were more specific it may help Kapil realise why he is anxious.'

Activity

Look at the following statements and have a go at rewriting them in a constructive and positive way.

- *That's not right, do it again.*

- *Oh no, you've made the same mistake as before, don't you ever learn?*

- *Well done.*

- *No, no, no, we've got a deadline to meet, get it done again and be quick.*

You will have noticed that most of the statements are very negative, and don't really help the student understand what they have done wrong and what they need to do to improve. If something was done well, say exactly what it was that was good about it. It is essential to be specific when giving feedback and it is a skill that takes a lot of practice.

Reviewing progress

It is important to review your students' progress regularly, as this gives you the opportunity to discuss on a one-to-one basis how they are progressing, and what they may need to improve or work on in the future. Often, this is formally recorded during tutorial sessions and signed by both parties so that records are maintained of the discussion.

At the time of reviewing progress, you may also revise or update the student's assessment plan. Reviews are a good opportunity to carry out formative assessments in an informal way. They also give the student the chance to ask questions they might have been embarrassed about asking in a group situation.

Keeping records

You need to keep records of how your students are progressing. If you mark a test or observe a task, how can you prove your student has achieved something if they lose their work? Each time you mark or assess your students' work, complete an individual feedback record of your decisions. This will show:

- who was assessed;

- what was assessed;

- when assessment took place;

- where assessment took place;

- why assessment took place;

- how assessment took place.

It should also identify any action that may be required. Once this action is complete, it should be noted.

You may find it useful to keep a tracking sheet of all your students' progress. A tracking sheet is simply a list of your students' names, with columns next to them indicating the date of assessment and grade or pass/refer for each topic or unit. This gives you an overview of all your students' progress. Original records are usually kept by you for a certain time for audit purposes. If you maintain computerised records, always ensure you follow relevant legislation.

Standardisation

If more than one person is delivering and/or assessing your course/qualification, it is important you all agree how you are making your decisions and why. It is useful to meet together and bring along examples of your assessment decisions to compare with others. You should be able to agree with the other assessors; if not, you will have to reach a suitable outcome based around the syllabus or course/qualification requirements. Standardisation enables consistency and fairness of assessment decisions.

Quality assurance

This is a way of confirming you are assessing and making decisions correctly. Usually, another member of staff who is qualified and experienced in your subject area will re-assess a sample of your work. They will be able to confirm your judgements, or give you advice if not. This is often known as *internal verification* and if a problem is found with a student's work, they have the chance to correct it. Another form of quality assurance is *internal moderation*. With this method, if the internal moderator finds problems with a particular area sampled, all the students' work for this particular area will need to be re-checked by the assessor.

You may also be observed by your internal verifier whilst you carry out assessments and they may talk to your students about the assessment process. The internal verifier will check your records and follow an audit trail of your dates of assessment, another reason for keeping your records up to date. If you are assessing towards a course with a qualification issued by an awarding body, you may also be visited by an external verifier who will check your records.

Activity

To help you reflect on the whole process of assessment, think about your own subject specialism and answer the following:

What are the best methods of assessment I could use and why?

Would I need to carry out an initial assessment?

Could I use formative and/or summative assessment methods of assessment?

How could I ensure my methods and decisions are valid and reliable?

What records would I keep and why?

Summary

In this chapter you have covered:

- What is assessment?
- Why assess?
- Initial assessment;
- Independent assessment;
- Formative/summative assessment;
- Planning assessment;
- Methods of assessment;
- Validity and reliability;
- Questioning techniques;
- Making assessment decisions;
- Giving feedback;
- Reviewing progress;
- Keeping records;
- Standardisation;
- Quality assurance.

Theory focus
Books

Tummons J (2005) *Assessing Learning in Further Education*, Learning Matters Ltd.

Publications

Assessing NVQs (1998) QCA.
Joint Awarding Body Guidance on Internal Verification of NVQs (1998) QCA.
NVQ Code of Practice (2001) QCA.

Websites

Disability Rights Commission – drc.gb.org

Equal Opportunities Commission – eoc.org.uk

Health and Safety Executive – hse.gov.uk

Lifelong Learning UK (LLUK) – lifelonglearninguk.org

Introduction

In this chapter you will cover the following points.

- Course evaluation;
- Self-evaluation, reflective practice and journals;
- Continuing professional development (CPD);
- Being professional;
- Responding to change.

There are activities and examples to help you reflect on the above which will assist your understanding of the evaluation process. Appendix 3 is a useful learning journal pro-forma that you may like to use to evaluate your learning.

This chapter contributes towards the knowledge and skills required for the City & Guilds 7302 Certificate in Delivering Learning: An Introduction:

→ Unit 3 – Delivery of a micro-teaching session

→ Unit 4 – Learning journal and summative profile.

This chapter contributes towards the knowledge and skills required for the City & Guilds 7302 Diploma in Delivering Learning:

→ Unit 5 – Communication, delivery and managing disruption: micro-teaching

→ Unit 6 – Observation and evaluation of an experienced teacher/trainer

→ Unit 7 – Professional development

→ Unit 8 – Professional practice – teaching/training

→ Unit 9 – Professional practice – case study.

This chapter contributes towards the knowledge and understanding required for the National Vocational Qualification (NVQ) in Learning and Development Level 3:

→ G3 – Evaluate and develop own practice

→ L16 – Monitor and review progress with learners

→ L18 – Respond to changes in learning and development.

This chapter contributes towards the knowledge and skills required for the International City & Guilds Certificate and Diploma in Teaching and Supporting Learners:

→ Unit 5 – Evaluation.

Course evaluation

You may be delivering a one-day programme, a short course of evening classes or a longer course leading to a qualification. Whichever type of course you deliver, it is important to evaluate the learning process. This will help you realise how effective you were and what you could improve in the future. It will also help you identify any problem areas, enabling you to do things differently next time. To do this, you could obtain feedback from your students in the form of a questionnaire. You may also get feedback from colleagues, your supervisor or inspectors who may observe your delivery.

If you have delivered a one-day programme or a short course, you might give your students a questionnaire at the end. Always build in time to your session for this to take place, otherwise your students will take away the questionnaire and forget to return it. It could contain closed questions such as: 'Were the delivery methods suitable? Yes/No,' or open questions such as: 'How did you find the delivery methods?'

If you are delivering a longer course, it is useful to obtain feedback part-way through the course, as well as at the end. This will enable you to make any necessary changes. Never assume everything is going well just because you think it is. You need feedback from your students to confirm they are enjoying their learning experience with you.

Activity

Imagine you are delivering a course of evening classes which lasts three terms. You have decided to obtain feedback by giving a short questionnaire to your students at the end of each term. What information would like to know after each term? How could you put this into a questionnaire?

You may have decided to use a mixture of open and closed questions. You may also decide to ask questions relating to your subject, the organisation and the environment.

Whatever you decide to ask, make sure you analyse the responses and do something about your findings.

Talking to your students informally will help you realise how successful your delivery has been. This can be done during reviews, at break times or before or after your session. Your students are the best judges of whether they are getting what they feel they need. They may give you more constructive feedback in an informal situation.

If you are delivering learning to employees in their place of work, you may like to obtain feedback from their employers to check that their newly acquired skills and knowledge have been put into practice successfully. If the employees are working towards a qualification, the employer will want to know the success rates. If some of the employees did not achieve, the employer will want to know why. You would need to make an evaluation as to whether it was your delivery methods or other factors that led to this.

Your organisation may make an evaluation of your course, perhaps to decide if it should be offered again in the future. They may make this decision based upon the number of students recruited to the course, their attendance patterns and whether they obtained a qualification at the end. They may contact students who dropped out of the course to find out why.

You may have to write a course report which your organisation will use as a basis to make a decision about the future. This report may include statistics such as how many students started, how many dropped out and how many achieved the qualification. This is known as *retention* and *achievement*, and you may have been set targets at the beginning of the course. If the targets are not met, your course may not be offered again.

Example

Li Han has delivered a course in flower arranging for the past five years as part of an adult and community initiative. Students paid an enrolment fee of £5 each for the course, which lasted six weeks, one evening per week. The course was delivered in a local village hall. All 15 places were taken, but some students dropped out as no formal qualification was offered. The room hire, resources and wages costs are too high to offer the course again in future. The adult community centre has not been able to secure any funding and has therefore decided not to offer this course again in the future.

Funding for some courses can be obtained from various external bodies. However, some courses may only be offered again if external funding can be obtained. The decision may be taken to modify your course, based upon student or employer feedback, to one that leads to a qualification which can attract funding.

Self-evaluation, reflective practice and journals

When delivering learning to others, you are also learning about yourself. For example, how you react to different situations or students, how patient you are and what skills you may need to develop. You may also decide you need further training to improve your knowledge and skills. You may have heard the saying 'You learn by your mistakes'. You may make mistakes – most people do. However, your students may not notice these. Although you will notice, you can ensure you don't make the same mistakes again in the future.

Activity

Imagine you have just delivered a one-day seminar to a group of company employees. How would you evaluate yourself?

You could use the following checklist based upon the training cycle. Answering all the questions will enable you to improve yourself and the experience you give to your students in the future. You may like to add further questions yourself.

- Identifying needs and planning – did I prepare a suitable session plan based upon the needs of the organisation, the syllabus and the students? Did I state my aims clearly to the group? Did I adhere to my session plan? How will I change the session plan for next time?

- Designing – did I arrive early to prepare the environment and equipment in advance? Did I use suitable delivery methods, resources and interesting handouts? Were these effective? What will I do differently next time?

- Facilitating – did I take into account the students' different learning styles? Did I give a clear introduction and summarise the subject regularly? Was my rate of presentation too fast or slow. Was my voice projection alright? Did I give out too many facts or use too much jargon? Was there a balance between tutor and student involvement? Did I encourage the students to ask questions? Was there mutual respect and trust? Did I treat all students as individuals, using their names and taking into account any additional needs? Did the group get along together? Was I in control of the session? Did I dress suitably? Was my body language and use of non-verbal expressions acceptable? Did I give a clear conclusion? What will I change next time?

- Assessing – did I assess the students during and at the end of the session to ensure they had learnt the necessary skills and knowledge? Do I need to do this differently next time?

● Evaluating – were there any unforeseen circumstances I had to deal with? Did I carry out all the relevant administrative and organisational requirements? Did I obtain feedback from the students? What will I do with this feedback?

Self-evaluation is crucial for your own development. After each session you deliver, think about how it went, what was good and why, and what could you improve or change? These are known as strengths and areas for development. Just ask yourself how you felt about the whole process. You may have a gut feeling that everything went well, but this is only your point of view. You need feedback from your students to confirm this.

If you have been attending a course yourself, you may have been keeping a learning journal, which will help you reflect on how your learning has informed a change in your attitudes and behaviour. Appendix 3 is a useful learning journal pro-forma that you may like to use to evaluate your learning.

Your organisation may have an appraisal or review process that you will have to participate in. This will involve others giving you feedback as well as you evaluating yourself. You may need to learn how to accept criticism and take it as constructive feedback about your professional role, not as something personal about yourself. As a result, you may need to adapt your delivery or attend further training in the light of changes in professional practices and subject expertise.

Activity

Thinking about the subject you wish to deliver, list the qualities and skills you feel you need to develop. How will you achieve these?

You might feel you need to develop your communication skills further; for example, you often say 'erm' when starting a sentence. You didn't know you did this until one of your students gave you feedback. You might therefore decide to make a visual recording of one of your sessions in order to view it later to see what might cause you to do this.

The process of self-reflection and your own further development should help improve the quality of service you give to your students.

Continuing professional development

Continuing your professional development throughout your career will ensure you are up to date with the latest information regarding your subject. You may need to keep records of this to satisfy an awarding or external body. Depending upon the subject you deliver, some external bodies require you to carry out several relevant activities per year. You may then need to write a reflective statement about how the activity has informed your learning and practice.

Activity

Thinking about the subject you wish to deliver, what do you need to do to ensure you are up to date? Are there any courses available locally or journals you could read? You could create an action plan for yourself, noting what you need to do, how you will do this and setting yourself target dates for achievement.

It is useful to subscribe to relevant journals, magazines, electronic updates from relevant websites, research the Internet and read books to keep up to date with changes in your subject.

Some awarding and external bodies require you to have the qualification you are delivering, either to the same level or to the level above that which you deliver.

Example

Pauline is delivering the National Vocational Qualification (NVQ) unit for new assessors, known as A1 – Assess candidates using a range of methods. For her to assess her students, she must hold the A1 award herself and carry out two relevant professional activities per year.

Being professional

As a tutor, you are a professional working within a value base and a code of professional practice set by your organisation and/or an external body.

Your students not only learn about the subject you deliver, but learn other things from you. This can be by the way you dress, act, respond to questions, offer support, etc. Your students don't need to know anything personal about you, but will probably make assumptions about you. If asked personal questions, try not to give out any information. By remaining a professional, and not becoming too friendly, you will retain their respect.

You need to add value to your delivery, be passionate about your subject and deliver it in an interesting way which will keep your students motivated.

Activity

How do you think a tutor should behave when delivering learning?

You may have responded by stating they should be professional, but defining what you consider to be professional might be a little more difficult. This could be that the tutor should be an expert at their subject, treat all students fairly, have a structure to their delivery with clear aims and targets, maintain control and avoid confrontation.

Being professional should include the following:

- dressing and acting appropriately;
- being organised with planning and delivery;
- arriving early to prepare the venue;
- preparing useful resources;
- having a contingency plan in case something goes wrong;
- allowing time for student and course reviews;
- leaving the venue tidy after your delivery, perhaps involving your students in this.

Being a professional is not just about the time you spend with your students. It includes all the other roles that go with teaching, for example:

- completing attendance records;
- maintaining records of student progress;
- standardising your practice with others;
- attending meetings;
- preparing delivery material and marking work;
- attending promotional events and exhibitions;
- referring students to other people or agencies when necessary.

Responding to change

In education, change is inevitable. Qualifications are updated by the regulatory authorities every few years and the curriculum and training needs of your organisation change in response to market needs.

Your organisation may be inspected by an external and/or funding body and they may find areas requiring improvement. There are also government, local and national debates and initiatives that would have an impact upon your role and profession.

You may need to update your literacy, numeracy and information technology (IT) skills. All this will help ensure you are a professional in your subject area.

Summary

In this chapter you have covered:

- Course evaluation;

- Self-evaluation, reflective practice and journals;

- Continuing professional development (CPD);

- Being professional;

- Responding to change.

Theory focus

Books

Francis M, Gould J (2000) *Fast Track to Training: A practical guide to successful teaching and training*, A-Train Publishing.

Reece I, Walker S (2003) *Teaching, Training and Learning*, 5th edition, Business Education Publishers Ltd.

Wallace S (2005) *Teaching and Supporting Learning in Further Education*, 2nd edition, Learning Matters Ltd.

Websites

Adult Learning Inspectorate – ali.gov.uk

Awdurdod Cymwysterau, Cwricwlwm ac Asesu Cymru – accac.org.uk

Council for the Curriculum, Examinations and Assessment in Northern Ireland – ccea.org.uk

Department for Education and Skills – dfes.gov.uk and teachernet.gov.uk

English and Maths online testing – move-on.org.uk

Learning and Skills Network – lsneducation.org.uk – lsda.org.uk

Lifelong Learning UK (LLUK) – lifelonglearninguk.org

Lifelong Learning – lifelonglearning.co.uk

National Institute of Adult Continuing Education – niace.org.uk

National Programme for Specialist Leaders of Behaviour and attendance – teachernet.gov.uk/wholeschool/behaviour/npsl_ba/

Office for Standards in Education – ofsted.gov.uk

Qualifications and Curriculum Authority – qca.org.uk

Scottish Qualifications Authority – sqa.org.uk

Sector Skills Development Agencies – ssda.org.uk

Support for Learning – support4learning.org.uk

Times Educational Supplement – tes.co.uk

ACCAC	Awdurdod Cymwysterau, Cwricwlwm ac Asesu Cymru. Qualifications, Curriculum and Assessment Authority for Wales
ALI	Adult Learning Inspectorate
APEL	Accreditation of Prior Experience and Learning
APL	Accreditation of Prior Learning
CCEA	Council for the Curriculum, Examinations and Assessment
CGLI	City & Guilds of London Institute
CPD	Continuing Professional Development
CRE	Commission for Racial Equality
DDA	Disability Discrimination Act
DfES	Department for Education and Skills
DRC	Disability Rights Commission
ELWA	Education and Learning Wales
ENTO	Employment National Training Organisation
EOC	Equal Opportunities Commission
EU	European Union
FE	Further Education
FENTO	Further Education National Training Organisation
FfA	Framework for Achievement
GCSE	General Certificate of Secondary Education
GNVQ	General National Vocational Qualification
HSE	Health and Safety Executive
ICT	Information Communication Technology
ILP	Individual Learning Plan
ILT	Information Learning Technology
IT	Information Technology

LLUK	Lifelong Learning UK
LSC	Learning and Skills Council
LSN	Learning and Skills Network
NIACE	National Institute of Adult Continuing Education
NLN	National Learning Network
NQF	National Qualifications Framework
NTO	National Training Organisation
NVQ	National Vocational Qualification
Ofsted	Office for Standards in Education
OHP	Overhead projector
PCET	Post Compulsory Education and Training
PGCE	Post Graduate Certificate in Education
QCA	Qualifications and Curriculum Authority
QTLS	Qualified Teacher Learning and Skills
SMART	Specific, Measurable, Achievable, Realistic, Time bound
SQA	Scottish Qualifications Authority
SSC	Sector Skills Council
SSDA	Sector Skills Development Agencies
SVUK	Standards Verification UK
TES	*Times Educational Supplement*
UK	United Kingdom
VACSR	Valid, Authentic, Current, Sufficient, Reliable
VAK	Visual, Aural, Kinaesthetic
VQ	Vocational Qualification
WBL	Work Based Learning
WWWWWWH	Who, What, When, Where, Why and How

Cross-referencing to Level 3 Standards

Chapter	City & Guilds Certificate in Delivering Learning: An Introduction	City & Guilds Diploma in Delivering Learning	NVQ L3 Learning and Development	International Certificate and Diploma in Teaching and Supporting Learners
1 Introduction	1, 2, 5	2, 7	L9	1, 3
2 Key principles of learning	1	1, 9	L9, L12, L13, L18	1
3 Identifying needs and planning learning	2, 3	2, 5, 8, 9	L3, L4, L5, L6, L10, L12, L13, L15	1, 2, 3
4 Designing learning	3	3, 5, 8, 9	L6, L7	2, 3
5 Facilitating learning	3	5, 6, 8	L9, L10, L11, L12, L13, L14	3
6 Assessing learning	3	4, 5	A1, A2, L3, L16, L20	1, 4
7 Evaluating learning	3, 4	5, 6, 7, 8, 9	G3, L16, L18	5

Checklist for delivering learning

Identifying needs and planning learning

Do I ... ?

- Have a syllabus/course guide

- Know when I will be delivering and for how long

- Have clear aims and objectives

- Have a scheme of work

- Have a session plan

- Need to devise learning activities, assessments and resources

- Plan to use a product or process model of delivery

- Know anything about my students that might affect my delivery or their learning

- Have an induction checklist

- Have an appropriate icebreaker or energiser

- Need to arrange refreshments or parking facilities

- Need to send out any pre-course information

Designing learning

Do I ... ?

- Know which room I will be delivering in

- Need to obtain any specialist equipment

- Need any further training myself

- Need to know any organisational procedures, e.g. health and safety, fire exits

- Need to find out where facilities such as the toilets are

- Have a contingency plan in case anything goes wrong

- Need to prepare the learning environment in any way

- Need to carry out an initial assessment with the students

- Need to carry out learning styles tests with the students

- Need to create any resources

- Need to check spelling, grammar and punctuation of my presentations

Facilitating learning
Can I ... ?

- Rehearse the session beforehand
- Ensure the environment is suitable, e.g. heating, lighting, ventilation, seating arrangements and disability access
- Arrive early to set up and check equipment, obtain pens, etc.
- Use a variety of delivery methods, activities and resources
- Mix formal and informal delivery in an appropriate manner
- Help agree ground rules
- Manage behaviour and disruption as it occurs
- Take any additional needs into consideration
- Support my students if the need arises
- Leave my personal problems behind
- Ask open questions
- Stipulate the times of breaks
- Allow time for questions at the end
- Keep attendance records

Assessing learning
Can I ... ?

- Assess students on an individual basis
- Ensure the validity and reliability of any assessment methods I use
- Give feedback to students on an individual basis in a positive and constructive manner
- Review student progress
- Keep records of progress

Evaluating learning
Did I ... ?

- Deliver an introduction, main content and summary
- Establish and maintain a rapport, putting students at ease
- Project energy and enthusiasm
- Have a structured approach
- Remain in control

- Take into account entitlement, equality, inclusivity and diversity of all students
- Behave in a professional manner
- Appear confident
- Have a positive attitude
- Use eye contact
- Use individual names
- Fidget or fiddle with anything
- Listen to my students
- Answer questions appropriately
- Recap key points regularly
- Dress appropriately
- Use appropriate body language and non-verbal communication
- Use any jargon or acronyms
- Achieve my aim
- Enjoy my delivery, if not, why not
- Deal with any difficult or unexpected situations appropriately
- Reflect on the session to develop my future delivery

Learning journal

Name:	Date:

The main points I have learnt from this session are:

How I could develop my delivery as a result of this learning:

How I could develop my knowledge as a result of this learning:

Scheme of work

Tutor

Qualification/Subject	Group	
Number of sessions	Delivery hours	Venue
Aim of programme		

Dates	Objectives/learning outcomes	Activities and resources	Assessment

Session plan

Tutor		Date		Room	
Subject		Time		Duration	
Aim of session					

Timing	Objectives/learning outcomes	Resources	Tutor activities	Learner activities	Assessments

Strengths	Areas for development	Action and improvements required

INDEX